WELCOME TO UEFA EURO 2024

ALEKSANDER ČEFERIN
UEFA PRESIDENT

Since its kick-off in 1960, the European Football Championship has become one of the planet's most thrilling sports events. This summer's edition has more than lived up to that billing, with 24 teams contributing to a wonderful festival of football as they aimed to make history and lift the much-desired Henri Delaunay trophy.

Famous for its rich footballing heritage, Germany has provided the perfect stage to host UEFA EURO 2024, a joyous occasion for players, officials and fans alike.

This summer's tournament has celebrated not just the skill and virtue of the protagonists on the field but also life, inclusion, and diversity.

UEFA, the German Football Association (DFB), and federal and local government structures have united to deliver an event honouring democracy, respect, tolerance, and human rights. We have taken significant steps to minimise the tournament's environmental impact and established a climate fund for grassroots football, which promises a lasting legacy.

I want to thank everyone involved, from our sponsors and partners to suppliers, for your incredible support and unwavering dedication to our mission.

Now, let's enjoy the final act of this magical summer of football in a spirit of fair play and respect, creating yet more unforgettable memories together.

Let's be united by football!

Seit ihrer ersten Ausgabe im Jahr 1960 hat sich die Fußball-Europameisterschaft zu einem der weltweit bekanntesten und spannendsten Sportereignisse hervorgetan. Das war diesen Sommer nicht anders – 24 Mannschaften sind angetreten, um den begehrten Henri-Delaunay-Pokal zu gewinnen, und haben uns ein denkwürdiges Fußballfest bereitet.

Gastgeber Deutschland, eine Fußballnation sondergleichen, bot die perfekte Bühne für die UEFA EURO 2024 und ihre Hauptakteure – die Spieler, Offiziellen und Fans. Das Turnier hat nicht nur das Können der Akteure, sondern auch die verschiedensten Aktivitäten abseits des Spielfelds rund um Inklusion und Vielfalt in den Fokus gerückt.

Die UEFA, der Deutsche Fußball-Bund (DFB) sowie die Bundesregierung, die Landesregierungen und die Städte haben gemeinsam eine Veranstaltung auf die Beine gestellt, die als Vorbild für Demokratie, Respekt, Toleranz und Menschenrechte gilt. Wir haben weitreichende Maßnahmen ergriffen, um die die Auswirkungen des Turniers auf die Umwelt zu minimieren, und einen Klimafonds für den Breitenfußball aufgelegt, der über den Sommer hinaus ein nachhaltiges Vermächtnis hinterlässt.

Ich möchte allen Beteiligten, von unseren Sponsoren und Partnern bis hin zu unseren Zulieferern, für ihr herausragendes Engagement und die tatkräftige Unterstützung unserer Arbeit danken.

Lassen Sie uns nun den letzten Akt dieses magischen Fußballsommers im Sinne von Fairplay und Respekt genießen und gemeinsam noch mehr unvergessliche Erinnerungen schaffen.

United by Football. Vereint im Herzen Europas.

WELCOME ALL

Everyone has a place in football

#FOOTBALL

UEFA

WELCOME

WILLKOMMEN IN DEUTSCHLAND

BERND NEUENDORF
DFB PRESIDENT

This summer, after a 36-year hiatus, Germany and the German Football Association have once again hosted a European Championship – all over Germany this time. Back in 1988, the only other time the European Championship was held here, our country was still divided. This year, alongside newcomers Dortmund in the west, and Leipzig and Berlin in the east, a total of ten cities have hosted the event. After weeks of incredible matches, our united Germany is now looking forward to the all-important final.

UEFA EURO 2024 has once again proved that Germany is a football-loving nation. The unifying power of our sport has been felt everywhere this summer, since the very first day of the tournament. In the stadiums and on the fan miles, supporters from all over the world have met and celebrated football peacefully together. We have witnessed some impressive fan marches and a cheerful and exuberant atmosphere in the host cities. Millions of people have also followed their teams on TV – cheering, celebrating and crying. That's the beauty of football.

UEFA EURO 2024 will have an impact long after the final, not only because of the lasting memories created by the outstanding teams and unique atmosphere, but because the tournament has also brought sustainability to the fore and given amateur football a real boost in a variety of ways.

All that remains if for me to wish you, and indeed all of us, an unforgettable final, replete with exciting football and inspiring encounters both inside and outside the stadiums.

Nach 36 Jahren durften Deutschland und der Deutsche Fußball-Bund in diesem Sommer wieder eine Europameisterschaft ausrichten – und zwar in ganz Deutschland. 1988, als die Europameisterschaft zum bisher einzigen Mal in Deutschland stattfand, war unser Land noch geteilt. In diesem Jahr zählten – neben dem Neuling Dortmund im Westen – Leipzig und Berlin im Osten erstmals zu unseren insgesamt zehn EM-Spielorten. Das wiedervereinte Deutschland freut sich nach großartigen Turnierwochen nun auf das große Finale.

Die UEFA EURO 2024 hat einmal mehr unter Beweis gestellt, dass Deutschland ein fußballbegeistertes Land ist. Die verbindende Kraft unseres Sports ist in diesem Sommer seit dem ersten Turniertag überall zu spüren. In den Stadien und auf den Fanmeilen sind sich Fans aus aller Welt begegnet und haben friedlich gemeinsam den Fußball gefeiert. Wir haben beeindruckende Fanmärsche und in den Host-Cities eine fröhliche und ausgelassene Stimmung erlebt. Und auch vor den Bildschirmen haben Millionen von Menschen Tag für Tag zusammen mit ihren Teams gefiebert, gejubelt und auch gelitten. Das ist Fußball.

Die UEFA EURO 2024 wird auch über das Finale hinaus langfristig wirken. Nicht nur, weil hochklassige Spiele und eine einzigartige Stimmung schon jetzt für bleibende Erinnerungen gesorgt haben. Die EURO hat darüber hinaus auch beim Thema Nachhaltigkeit klare Akzente gesetzt und wird den Amateurfußball durch verschiedene Maßnahmen und Projekte voranbringen. Ich wünsche Ihnen und uns allen ein großartiges Finale mit begeisterndem Fußball und inspirierenden Begegnungen im und außerhalb des Stadions.

CONTENTS

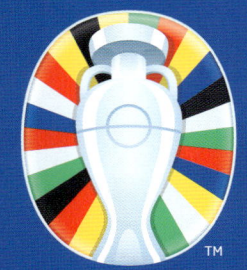

UEFA EURO 2024 GERMANY

CONTENTS

10 ANGELOS CHARISTEAS INTERVIEW

18 SEMI-FINAL ACTION & ROAD TO THE FINAL

28 FOCUS ON THE FINALISTS

36 HENRI DELAUNAY: THE MAN BEHIND THE TROPHY

42 OLYMPIASTADION BERLIN

47 THE MATCHES THAT DECIDED THE TROPHY'S DESTINY

CONTENTS

78

66 THE HISTORIC CITY OF BERLIN

78 1988: GULLIT, HISTORY AND 'THAT' GOAL

68 A PARTY IN GERMANY: THE PICTURES THAT PROVE IT

89 HOW TO WIN A EURO: MANCINI INTERVIEW

EDITORIAL
Editor: Roy Gilfoyle
Lead designer: Adam Ward
Designer: Neil Haines
Sub editors: Simon Monk, Adam Oldfield, Peter Leathley, Peter Milby, Adrian Caffery, Scott Squires, Jonah Webb

FOR UEFA
Sam Adams, Emmanuel Deconche, Christophe Burri, Lars Bretscher, James Raybaudo, Thomas Sauvage, Jim Agnew, Andrin Cooper, Peter Dennis, Stephen Mines, Dominique Maurer, Arona Gaye

REACH SPORT
Content sales director: Fergus McKenna
Head of commercial partnerships: David Scripps
Commissioning editor: Chris Brereton
Operations manager: Nick Moreton
Marketing & communications manager: Claire Brown

PHOTOGRAPHY
UEFA, Alamy

OFFICIAL LICENSED PRODUCT PUBLISHED BY
Reach Sport

PRINTED BY
Buxton Press

A TOBACCO-FREE TOURNAMENT
A no-smoking policy is in operation at UEFA EURO 2024. Thank you for respecting the no-smoking policy and enjoy the games.

© UEFA EURO 2024. All rights reserved. The UEFA EURO 2024 words, the UEFA EURO 2024 logo and the UEFA EURO 2024 trophy are protected by trademarks and/or copyright of UEFA. All rights reserved. No use for commercial purposes may be made of such trademarks. Printed under licence by Reach Sport.
This programme is sold subject to the condition that it may not be reproduced, stored in a retrieval system or transmitted on any form or by any means, electronic, mechanical, photocopying, recording or otherwise, without prior consent. No part of this publication may be reproduced without the written permission of the copyright owners. Every effort has been made by the publishers to ensure the accuracy of this publication; the publishers cannot accept responsibility for errors or omissions. In the interest of independence and impartiality, many features in this publication have been written by third-party experts. Any opinions expressed therein are the views of the writers themselves and not necessarily those of UEFA and Reach Sport.
UEFA and Reach Sport can not be held responsible for changes to general team-related content, scheduling, venues, or any other circumstance changes that occurred since going to print.

UNIFYING POWER OF FOOTBALL

The tone was set right at the start of this tournament. Fans from across the continent created a euphoric party atmosphere, both inside and outside of the stadiums. This picture of supporters of Germany and Scotland from the first matchday shows how football, friendship and fun have mixed together perfectly over the past month.

INTERVIEW

ANGELOS CHARISTEAS

BRINGING JOY TO A NATION

TWENTY YEARS ON FROM ONE OF THE MOST REMARKABLE WINS IN EURO HISTORY, ANGELOS CHARISTEAS TAKES US THROUGH A TOURNAMENT THAT HELPED HIM ACHIEVE HIS CHILDHOOD DREAM

As you headed into UEFA EURO 2004, what were expectations like in Greece?
"Considering we were playing in a tournament in a country like Portugal, we were facing the hosts in our first match, and we had Spain in our group, nobody expected – us included – that we would make it past the first round.

"We expected to score a goal, maybe get a draw or win a game, perhaps against the Russians. But, under no circumstances did anyone expect us to get out of the group stage.

"That gave us extra motivation to make the Greeks proud and prove to ourselves that we travelled to Portugal to do more, to achieve something more spectacular."

ANGELOS CHARISTEAS

Then the finals began. You beat Portugal and drew against Spain. What did these matches do for self-confidence in the team?
"In these kinds of tournaments, I believe the first match is always very important. When we faced Portugal in the opening game on their home ground, you know that a positive result will boost your chances tenfold, as there are only three matches in the group stage.

"So, we won the first game, and we did so in style. We played good football and scored two beautiful goals. I believe it was at that point that the Greeks started believing. It doesn't take much for us Greeks to get excited, to believe and to become passionate.

"In our first game, we proved that we were serious contenders, that we went there to achieve something, and we weren't just there for a holiday. That is when people realised that this team had the passion and the fire to reach the next round."

The father of this achievement was Otto Rehhagel. What kind of coach was he?
"I definitely believe that our coach was one of the most important factors in our success.

"When a team has a very good selection of players, who play in big leagues, players with personality and talent, they need a coach who can get 100% out of them.

"Otto did manage to get 100% out of each one of us and, at the end of the day, he is one of Greece's most successful national team coaches. I believe that his story will forever be engraved in Greek hearts."

What was Greece's philosophy at the time – the system, the tactics?
"As Otto Rehhagel has always said, our system was 'economic attack'. That meant we always wanted to focus on our defence and, when given the opportunity, to be able to hit back at our rivals.

"I remember the match against Spain, in particular – our second in the group stage. Spain took the lead, but we found a way to equalise in a very tough encounter.

"I will not forget how we managed to hold onto the 1-1 result that day under very difficult circumstances. We proved there that our aim was always to defend proactively."

> "When a team has a very good selection of players, who play in big leagues, players with personality and talent, they need a coach who can get 100% out of them"

INTERVIEW

> "We felt the burden growing heavier on our shoulders. But at the same time self-confidence and strength were growing"

You scored three goals at the finals. What do you remember about these goals against Spain, against France in the quarter-finals and, of course, your goal in the final?
"I believe that the goal against Spain came at the right time, because Spain had taken the lead. It was very hard to get back into the game. I remember seeing Vasilios Tsiartas lift his head and whip in a great cross. For the first time [that afternoon] I had broken free from [Carlos] Puyol for a few metres. I was able to control the ball, shoot and beat Iker Casillas.

"The second goal was truly one of the best of my career. It was against France and started with a fantastic move on the right. [Theodoros] Zagorakis got past [Bixente] Lizarazu with a beautiful move and carved out an excellent cross.

"I had broken free from the opponents' marking by the penalty spot in France's box and scored one of my best goals with a header. That goal has become historic in Greece.

"The third goal, against Portugal, proved that set-pieces were always our strong point. We worked a lot on corners, free-kicks and we were very focused in dead-ball situations.

"Before Angelos Basinas took that corner, I remember looking at the crowd behind the goal. Those stands were filled with Greeks. I said to myself, 'This is the time to score a goal'. We managed to get the 1-0 and we won the EURO."

There was a real 'wow' moment in the quarter-finals when you beat France. Were you confident you could win that one?
"When we played France, we realised that things had moved up to another level. As far as we were concerned, we had already achieved success. Back home, everybody was saying that we had achieved our goal by getting out of the group stage at the EURO.

"We played against the best football team in the world at the time. They had players like Zinédine Zidane and Thierry Henry in their ranks – world-class players. We could only begin to think about achieving such a tremendous result.

"I believe that our best game in the EURO [2004] was against France. We faced the best team in the tournament and by beating France we proved that we had our sights on the final."

Having played against Portugal in your opening match, did that help you prepare for the final against the same opponents?
"We knew that winning our first game against the Portuguese was a shock for Portugal and for the whole country. We realised that over the next couple of weeks at the tournament.

"The final was a completely different game. We knew that the Portuguese were giving us respect. And secondly, we were nervous too because we were playing in the final and it was our biggest opportunity ever to win this prestigious trophy. So, it was a completely different game.

"We were counting on the fact that as the time passed and the score stayed at 0-0, the [Portuguese] players on the pitch and the whole country would start feeling anxious, would start seeing flashbacks to the first game they played against us.

"As the time passed, we felt that's what was happening and that's when we struck. On our side, our strength grew the longer we played, and we had the support of our fans.

"That's what we were counting on. That was our strategy which, in the end, helped us to lift the trophy."

Just before the final, there was an incredible amount of excitement back in Greece. How did that affect the mood in the squad?
"First of all, that was the time we couldn't see what was going on in Greece. We were only told on the phone by our families that the people in Greece were out in the streets.

"After the win against France, they started to talk about the final and potentially [winning] the trophy. We felt that the burden was growing heavier on our shoulders. But at the same time our self-confidence and our strength were growing, and we were receiving some great messages from the fans who were in Portugal.

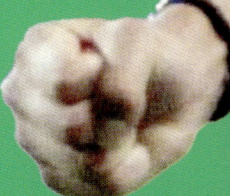

14 UEFA EURO 2024 OFFICIAL MATCHDAY PROGRAMME

ANGELOS CHARISTEAS

"I will never forget that, from the first game until the last, people were coming to Portugal from Greece and all over the world to see the national team play. That gave us a lot of strength and confidence. I'm happy that, in the end, we rewarded them with this joyous occasion."

In the first half, it was a very balanced game. What do you remember of it?
"It was a very tight game for us. We had very good, specific tactics on our side. We knew that the likes of Cristiano [Ronaldo], Figo and Rui Costa wanted to score as quickly as possible to give their team the lead.

"I remember that in the first half we were mostly being mindful defensively. But occasionally we went forward and showed that we could be dangerous and cause problems for the Portuguese.

"I would say that the first half passed very quickly because we were as nervous as the Portuguese and didn't want to make any mistakes and let our opponents score."

Then in the second half, you scored...
"I think that our team went down in history as the team which had scored the most goals from set-pieces. I remember Giourkas Seitaridis won a corner on the right. When we went up into the box to take our positions we were all thinking the same thing. We were thinking that it was our chance. And they were afraid because they had already seen what we could do from our game against the Czech Republic when we won with a last-gasp header from [Traianos] Dellas.

OFFICIAL PAYMENT PARTNER OF UEFA EURO 2024™

Kicking off the future**s** of global commerce

Visit antglobal.com

支 | Alipay+

Cross-border digital payment platform connecting 28 mobile apps and over 88 million merchants in 57 markets globally

antom

All-in-one platform to help merchants of all sizes collect payments and grow revenue from over 250 payment methods worldwide

WORLDFIRST

One-stop digital payment and financial services platform for global businesses, especially SMEs in international trade, with over 1m+ clients and 200bn+ USD in transactions

ANGELOS CHARISTEAS

"They saw the same fire in our eyes. I believe that psychology plays a very important role in these situations and psychologically we were feeling very good. We knew that we could seal the victory with one of these opportunities."

How did it feel to score that goal?
"From the age of eight I had dreamt of scoring an important goal for my national team, to make my parents and my country proud.
   "When I scored that goal, even today, I get emotional when I think about it. My childhood dream had come true. When you score that kind of goal, you realise that you've achieved your aim, your dream, that you've made your own people, your family and the whole country proud.
   "So, all these emotions, the joy of winning, the joy of football and that you've made your dream come true, came out on the field and on my face. I will never forget this moment."

And then the final whistle. How did you feel when you were presented with the trophy?
"We couldn't comprehend what we had just done, what we had achieved. We fell to the ground and cried with joy.
   "We saw fans in the stands shouting and crying with joy and pride. Greece is a small country with only 10 million people but it's a proud country with passionate people.
   "The people are passionate, and they were moved and proud. All these feelings came out for us and all Greeks."

How was it when you returned to Athens?
"The party went on for a long time, for many days. I remember that we didn't sleep for two or three days. When we arrived in Athens, we took a bus and the journey lasted five or six hours.
   "There were millions of people in the streets. Greeks with

"In the 20 years that have gone by I have heard countless stories. I feel so blessed. I have received so much love from people"

joy in their eyes. It was the best thing a football player can ever experience and I'm happy that I managed to be a part of that."

Twenty years on, what has stayed with you from that tournament?
"What always stays with you is the joy of lifting a trophy for your country. Truthfully, I don't really dwell on goals or on-pitch performances.
   "I was focusing on the Greeks all over the world on that day. In the 20 years that have gone by, I have heard countless stories. Thousands of stories... I feel so blessed. I have received so much love from people.
   "What has stayed in my memory most of all from EURO 2004 is that we were able to lift a whole country and brought Greeks out into the streets. No matter where they were, in America, Australia or elsewhere in the world, Greeks felt elated by that huge success. They were immensely proud.
   "I will not forget that, when we returned to Athens, all the people were waiting for us in Panathenaic Stadium. I will not forget the reception we got and, of course, I will never forget the fans in the stadium when the final against Portugal was over."

SEMI-FINAL ACTION

SEMI-FINAL ACTION

SEMI-FINAL ACTION

MUNICH

SPAIN 2
YAMAL 21, OLMO 25

FRANCE 1
KOLO MUANI 9

SPAIN:
Unai Simón, Jesús Navas (Vivian 58), Nacho, Laporte, Cucurella, Rodri, Fabián Ruiz, Yamal (Ferran Torres 90+3), Olmo (Merino 76), Williams (Zubimendi 90+3), Morata (Oyarzabal 76)

FRANCE:
Maignan, Koundé, Upamecano, Saliba, T. Hernández, Kanté (Griezmann 62), Tchouameni, Rabiot (Camavinga 62), Dembélé (Giroud 79), Kolo Muani (Barcola 62), Mbappé

Spain reached their fifth EURO final as a stunning goal from record-breaking teenager Lamine Yamal helped them come from behind against a disciplined and resolute French side.

After Randal Kolo Muani headed in Kylian Mbappé's early cross to give France the lead, it was Yamal's turn to underline his extraordinary prowess and maturity with a wonderful curling effort from outside the box.

At just 16 years and 362 days, he became the youngest ever scorer at a EURO tournament – and set his country up to go on and win this tight, enthralling occasion.

Just four minutes after Yamal's sensational equaliser, Dani Olmo scored his third goal at UEFA EURO 2024 to put Spain 2-1 in front – and that meant France had to try and get on the offensive.

They managed this several times, with Aurelien Tchouameni and Mbappé both going close for Didier Deschamps' side, but Spain showed plenty of defensive and tactical knowledge to see the game out safely. They will take some beating this evening.

SEMI-FINAL ACTION

"There is one step missing. It is unbelievable to be in the final. We deserve to be in this final. We're a step away from glory. It was unfortunate to fall a goal behind but we did not give up"

— Dani Olmo

SEMI-FINAL ACTION

"I'm very happy to have made it to the final. Now the most important thing is to win it. I'm very happy. I try not to think too much, enjoy it and help the team and if it works out like this, I'm happy"

— Lamine Yamal

"I have to keep my faith in this group of players. They always work for the common good. It's just another sign that this is an insatiable team. I'm proud to be able to direct these players"

— Luis de la Fuente

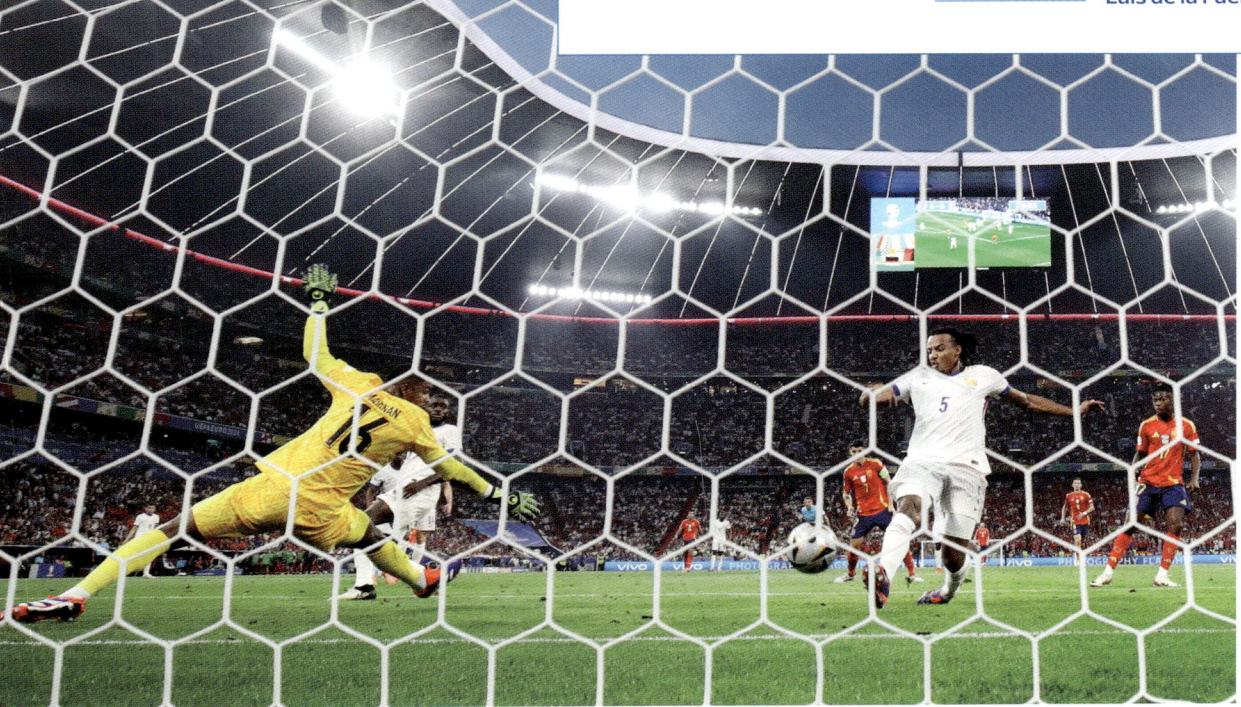

ROAD TO THE FINAL
SPAIN

GROUP STAGE

MATCH 1

SPAIN Morata 29, Fabián Ruiz 32, Carvajal 45+2	3
CROATIA	0

MATCH 2

SPAIN Calafiori (og) 55	1
ITALY	0

MATCH 3

ALBANIA	0
SPAIN Ferran Torres 13	1

ROUND OF 16

SPAIN Rodri 39, Fabián Ruiz 51, Williams 75, Olmo 83	4
GEORGIA Le Normand (og) 18	1

QUARTER-FINALS

SPAIN Olmo 51, Merino 119	2
GERMANY Wirtz 89	1

After extra time

SEMI-FINALS

SPAIN 2 v 1 **FRANCE**
Yamal 21, Olmo 25 — Kolo Muani 9

ROAD TO THE FINAL
ENGLAND

GROUP STAGE

MATCH 1

SERBIA	0
ENGLAND Bellingham 13	1

MATCH 2

DENMARK Hjulmand 34	1
ENGLAND Kane 18	1

MATCH 3

ENGLAND	0
SLOVENIA	0

ROUND OF 16

ENGLAND Bellingham 90+5, Kane 91	2
SLOVAKIA Schranz 25	1

After extra time

SEMI-FINALS

NETHERLANDS	1	v	2	ENGLAND
Simons 7				Kane (p) 18, Watkins 90+1

QUARTER-FINALS

ENGLAND Saka 80	1
SWITZERLAND Embolo 75	1

England win 5-3 on penalties

UEFA EURO 2024 OFFICIAL MATCHDAY PROGRAMME

SEMI-FINAL ACTION

SEMI-FINAL ACTION

SEMI-FINAL ACTION

DORTMUND

NETHERLANDS 1

SIMONS 7

ENGLAND 2

KANE (p) 18, WATKINS 90+1

NETHERLANDS:
Verbruggen, Dumfries (Zirkzee 90+3), De Vrij, Van Dijk, Aké, Schouten, Simons (Brobbey 90+3), Reijnders, Malen (Weghorst 46), Depay (Veerman 35), Gakpo

ENGLAND:
Pickford, Walker, Stones, Guéhi, Saka (Konsa 90+3), Mainoo (Gallagher 90+3), Rice, Trippier (Shaw 46), Foden (Palmer 81), Kane (Watkins 81), Bellingham

England needed to show confidence and character as they came from a goal down to beat the Netherlands and reach the country's first major tournament final on foreign soil.

In front of a colourful and vibrant crowd in Dortmund, Ronald Koeman's men struck first as Xavi Simons' rocket flew past Jordan Pickford from outside the area.

England didn't have long to wait to reply as Harry Kane converted a penalty 11 minutes later, hard and low to Bart Verbruggen's right.

An action-packed first half saw both sides strike the frame of the goal, Denzel Dumfries heading against the crossbar from a corner, while Phil Foden's long-range strike clipped the post.

Foden also had an effort cleared off the line but the decisive moment arrived in added time at the end of the second half. Substitutes Cole Palmer and Ollie Watkins linked up and the Aston Villa striker struck a ferocious shot through Stefan de Vrij's legs and into the far corner.

SEMI-FINAL ACTION

"We've delivered again. These moments are great. They bring us together as a team and as a family. It's about bringing that into the final"

— Jude Bellingham

SEMI-FINAL ACTION

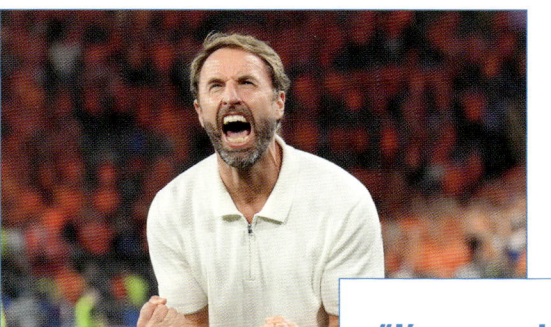

> "I've been waiting for that moment for weeks. I got the opportunity and took it with both hands. When it went in the bottom corner it was the best feeling ever"
>
> — Ollie Watkins

> "I'm so chuffed for Ollie to get his moment. To be able to take England to a first [major] final overseas, I'm immensely proud of that"
>
> — Gareth Southgate

THE FINALISTS

SPAIN

If major tournaments were won on style and the amount of high-quality attacking football played, many fans around the world would have handed the trophy to Spain already.

Of course, that isn't how football works and there is a final to be won, but Spain are a team that have impressed throughout UEFA EURO 2024.

Luis de la Fuente has crafted a team that has proven winners and experience in the likes of Dani Carvajal and Rodri, knowing they have mercurial players at the top end of the pitch that can hurt any team.

Álvaro Morata has been scoring goals at major tournaments for years, but now he has emerging superstars in Nico Williams and Lamine Yamal in the wide areas who are unfazed by the lofty stage they are performing on, while Dani Olmo has shown his class through the middle.

Spain are the only team to have scored in every game and win all their matches in Germany so far and they have created an aura of a side that knows it is good enough to win a EURO for the first time since they won back-to-back titles in 2008 and 2012.

In that era Spain would win admiration, as well as numerous matches, with a relentless passing style that controlled possession and exhausted opponents into submission. The team of today is more direct and has pace in key areas that their rivals struggle to deal with.

Their performance in the semi-final against France showed that they can beat the best sides in the world and deal with high-pressure situations. If they can do that one more time, Spain will become four-time EURO champions.

> "I know my players can give much more and be even better, and I'm pretty sure we will. We want to play to our strengths"
>
> — Luis de la Fuente

THE FINALISTS

EURO RECORD

1960	Withdrew
1964	Winners
1968	Did not qualify
1972	Did not qualify
1976	Did not qualify
1980	Group stage
1984	Runners-up
1988	Group stage
1992	Did not qualify
1996	Quarter-finals
2000	Quarter-finals
2004	Group stage
2008	Winners
2012	Winners
2016	Round of 16
2020	Semi-finals

TOP GOALSCORER
This tournament

DANI OLMO

3

THE COACH
LUIS DE LA FUENTE

There is no better person to be leading this collection of some of the most talented young players Spain has ever produced than Luis de la Fuente.

The Spain head coach may only have taken over in his current role following the 2022 FIFA World Cup but he was formerly in charge of Spain's Under-19, Under-21 and Under-23 squads so he has great knowledge of the talented players who are fast developing from being players for the future into players for now.

De la Fuente's expertise in guiding young footballers is playing out in front of our eyes as the likes of Lamine Yamal, Pedri and Nico Williams have put in great performances at this tournament.

The former Sevilla and Athletic Club defender replaced Luis Enrique as Spain head coach and has wasted little time in turning the side into a well-balanced team that gives little away but has plenty of attacking flair.

He already has a trophy under his belt, having guided Spain to become UEFA Nations League champions in 2023.

This tournament has seen De la Fuente gain even more admirers as Spain's stylish performances have caught the eye. And his reputation would reach even greater heights if victory is clinched tonight.

THE FINALISTS

PLAYER FOCUS

LAMINE YAMAL

Regular viewers of La Liga matches last season already knew what is becoming clear to the rest of us now, that Lamine Yamal – who turned 17 yesterday – is a young man that is ready to take on the world.

The Barcelona attacker had a sensational campaign in 2023/24 and Luis de la Fuente has already made him a pivotal player in his Spain attack.

When he made his major tournament debut against Croatia he became the youngest player ever to compete at a EURO at the age of 16 and it seemed only a matter of time before he would become the youngest ever goalscorer.

That moment arrived in spectacular style during the semi-final against France as he picked up the ball 25 metres from goal and curled a beautiful shot beyond a top-class goalkeeper in Mike Maignan.

STATS

6 GAMES

3 ASSISTS

NICO WILLIAMS

One of the jewels in the Spanish attacking crown is Athletic Club winger Nico Williams.

With fast feet, a box of tricks and the kind of unpredictable style that keeps opposition defenders constantly on their toes, Williams had a growing reputation before this EURO began that has only been enhanced since.

Operating on the opposite wing to Lamine Yamal, Williams, who turned 22 on Friday, has caught the eye with some fantastic performances and was Player of the Match in Spain's group-stage win over Italy.

A perfect example of what Williams is capable of came in the 4-1 win win against Georgia in the round of 16 when he breezed past the last defender and blasted high into the net – and he was on song again in the semi-final, causing France right-back Jules Koundé no end of problems.

STATS

5 GAMES

35.8 km/h TOP SPEED

DANI OLMO

With three goals and two assists to his name already, there's no doubting Dani Olmo's contribution to Spain's run to the final of UEFA EURO 2024.

When the tournament began, the Leipzig attacker had to settle for a place on the bench but his importance to the side has grown as the matches have come and gone and in the knockout rounds Olmo has been sensational.

He opened his account in the 4-1 round of 16 win against Georgia and was Player of the Match against Germany in the quarter-finals, slotting in Spain's opening goal and bending in a delightful cross for Mikel Merino's late winner.

In the semi-final he produced a goal of real class as his touch allowed him to find space in a packed area and blast in what turned out to be the winning goal. Does he have another knockout goal in his locker tonight?

STATS

3 GOALS

2 ASSISTS

OFFICIAL SMARTPHONE

X100 Series 5G
Co-engineered with ZEISS

Photography. Redefined.

THE FINALISTS

ENGLAND

If togetherness and team spirit are qualities needed to succeed at the top level of international sport then it's no surprise that England have given themselves this opportunity to play for the right to lift the Henri Delaunay Cup.

Such are the high hopes back home for this England team that despite their progress to Berlin for tonight's showpiece match, performances in the group stage certainly left their followers wanting more.

Undeterred, Gareth Southgate has formed a bond with his players that means they put every drop of effort into winning matches for their coach and the fans, and it has resulted in a path to the final that has gathered momentum with each passing game.

It is no wonder that there is such belief in this group of players.

In captain Harry Kane, England have one of world football's greatest goalscorers. He is ably assisted by attacking talents like Bukayo Saka, Phil Foden and Cole Palmer, while 21-year-old Jude Bellingham has catapulted himself into the same bracket as the globe's greatest players – especially since his overhead kick that saved the Three Lions against Slovakia in the round of 16.

The performances have continued to improve as England have grown into the tournament, with the semi-final victory against the Netherlands arguably resulting in their best showing at UEFA EURO 2024.

And the quarter-final win over Switzerland proved that should tonight's match go all the way to penalties, they have players who can handle the pressure.

> "We're here still — we're fighting, on the back of a really good performance [against the Netherlands]. I'm just so pleased for everybody back home"
>
> — Gareth Southgate

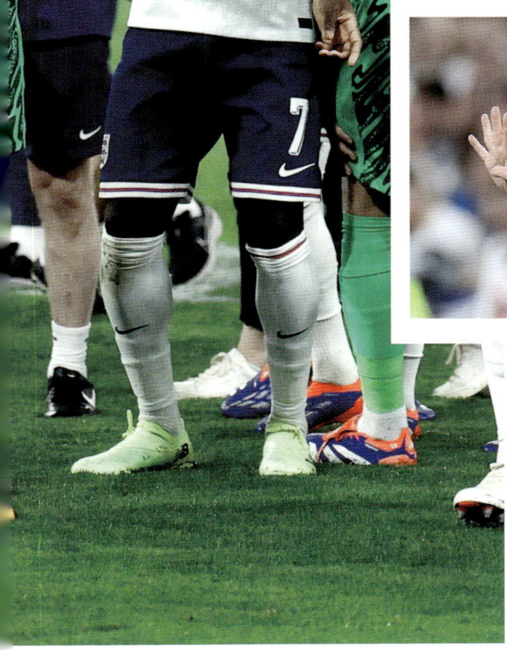

THE FINALISTS

EURO RECORD

1960	Did not enter
1964	Did not qualify
1968	Third place
1972	Did not qualify
1976	Did not qualify
1980	Group stage
1984	Did not qualify
1988	Group stage
1992	Group stage
1996	Semi-finals
2000	Group stage
2004	Quarter-finals
2008	Did not qualify
2012	Quarter-finals
2016	Round of 16
2020	Runners-up

TOP GOALSCORER
This tournament

HARRY KANE

3

THE COACH
GARETH SOUTHGATE

Calm and collected in the technical area he may be, but when England score or secure a big win, nobody is more animated than head coach Gareth Southgate.

After earning 57 caps as a player for his country, there was no-one more honoured to be given the responsibility of leading the Three Lions when he was handed his current role in 2016.

The England job comes with a huge weight of expectation as the country yearns for the opportunity of seeing their national team win a major trophy for the first time since 1966.

Consistent qualification for major tournaments has become the norm under Southgate, and reaching the knockout rounds has become a regular occurrence.

The 2018 and 2022 FIFA World Cups saw semi-final and quarter-final finishes respectively, and at UEFA EURO 2020 England came painfully close to claiming the Henri Delaunay Cup for the first time, following Italy's penalty shoot-out victory at Wembley.

England's route to the final this year hasn't been straightforward following a series of hard-fought matches. But England have reached the final for the second successive EURO, and if they can go one final step, Southgate will become a national hero.

THE FINALISTS

PLAYER FOCUS

JUDE BELLINGHAM

In a EURO that has been full of big names and top performances, a select few can claim to be true global stars but Jude Bellingham is among them.

The midfield all-rounder made his Birmingham City debut aged 16, and four years later had played for Borussia Dortmund before signing for Real Madrid. His meteoric rise also included a debut for England at the age of 17, and now 21 he is already playing in his third major tournament.

Every challenge that has been thrown at him, Bellingham has excelled at, which is no surprise when he appears to have no weaknesses in his game.

And if big moments are the mark of a player, his winner against Serbia and spectacular overhead kick against Slovakia to keep England in the tournament prove that Bellingham is up there with the best.

STATS

6 GAMES

2 GOALS

KYLE WALKER

Since Gareth Southgate took the reins as England coach in 2016, Kyle Walker has been there every step of the way.

Walker was selected at right-back in that first game against Malta and he has been a big part of his manager's plans ever since, playing in every major tournament England have qualified for under Southgate's stewardship.

At UEFA EURO 2020, Walker's performances were such that he was named in the Team of the Tournament.

So far in this EURO, the 34-year-old has been as dependable as ever, whether operating at right-back or as one of three central defenders.

Whichever position he plays in and no matter which opponent he faces, Walker's pace and experience means he is one of the toughest defenders to get the better of – and he shows no signs of slowing down yet.

STATS

6 GAMES

34.8km/h TOP SPEED

HARRY KANE

When England have needed a big goal, the man most likely to supply it over the past few years has been Harry Kane.

The Bayern München striker, who enjoyed a prolific first season in the Bundesliga last year having signed from Tottenham, has scored goals regularly for his country since his spectacular international debut in 2015.

On that day he scored inside two minutes of being introduced as a substitute against Lithuania and he now has 66 goals, which makes him England's record goalscorer of all time.

The Golden Boot winner at the 2018 FIFA World Cup, this is Kane's fifth major tournament and he has scored three times – one each against Denmark, Slovakia and the Netherlands – during England's run to this final.

He would love to come up with the winning goal tonight.

STATS

6 GAMES

3 GOALS

Italy's Jorginho with the trophy named after the tournament's founding father, Henri Delaunay (inset). Opposite: the original version

HENRI DELAUNAY – THE MAN BEHIND THE TROPHY

Along with the FIFA World Cup, the best-known international football tournament on the planet is the UEFA European Championship.

It's been 64 years since the inaugural tournament – then known as the European Nations' Cup – took place in France in 1960. And there is one man who proved to be the catalyst for the competition becoming a reality.

Born in June 1883, Henri Delaunay was a French football administrator who had played a crucial role in the foundation of UEFA in 1954, and served as the organisation's first general secretary until his untimely death in November 1955.

Delaunay had dreamed of setting up a Europe-wide international competition since the 1920s. In 1927 he and Austrian football administrator Hugo Meisl submitted a proposal to world governing body FIFA for the creation of a European national team cup.

Sadly, Delaunay wouldn't live to see his ultimate goal come to fruition. Yet his name will forever be etched into the tournament's past, present and future.

At the launch of the competition in Stockholm in 1958, UEFA's first president, Ebbe Schwartz, proposed that in recognition of the Frenchman's influence in the creation of the tournament, the trophy awarded to the winning nation should carry his name.

The president of the French Football Federation, Pierre Pochonet, announced that his association would offer the trophy, and it fell to Delaunay's son Pierre to have the new silverware manufactured. Pierre Delaunay had succeeded his late father as UEFA general secretary in 1956 and continued the work to get the competition up and running.

The original trophy went on show for the first time at the four-team tournament in 1960 – which was won by the Soviet Union following a 2-1 victory (after extra time) against Yugoslavia – and would be lifted by winning captains 12 times.

As the EURO grew in size and stature, it was felt that the original trophy was too small in comparison to silverware for UEFA's other competitions, such as the Champions League.

UEFA wanted to improve on the quality and scale of the trophy and renowned London-based goldsmith, silversmith and jewellers Asprey were handed the job in the run-up to EURO 2008 in Austria and Switzerland.

There was no question about the name of the new silverware, however – it would continue to be known as the Henri Delaunay Cup.

Delaunay, of course, is not the only man to have a famous football trophy named after him. He was friends with fellow Frenchman Jules Rimet, whose name was given to the original FIFA World Cup trophy.

HENRI DELAUNAY

DNA OF **DEMOCRACY**

75 Jahre Grundgesetz

„AUCH DIE DIGITALE WÜRDE DES MENSCHEN IST UNANTASTBAR."

Lasst uns gemeinsam die Demokratie im Netz stärken. Werde Teil der Telekom Initiative „Gegen Hass im Netz".
Gemeinsam #GegenHassImNetz

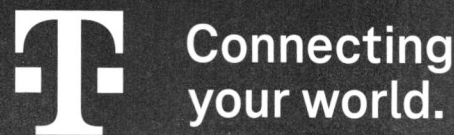

MEET THE MASCOT: ALBÄRT

One of the most instantly recognisable figures at this summer's tournament is Albärt: the official mascot for UEFA EURO 2024.

Given his name in a vote by children in UEFA's Football in Schools programme along with fans on UEFA.com, Albärt fought off competition from other bear-related shortlisted names such as Bärnardo, Bärnheart and Herzi von Bär.

The EURO mascot pays homage to the popular children's teddy bear toy, which is said to have originated in Germany in the early 20th century.

Albärt's debut was just over a year ago at a friendly match in Gelsenkirchen, where the national team faced Colombia. However, his first public appearance was earlier that day at a local primary school, showcasing his commitment to stirring up excitement about football among children across Europe.

He has continued to visit schools across Europe and also joined forces with Germany's football star Jamal Musiala, taking on the role of 'Substitute Teacher' in a series of EURO-themed lessons and challenges. These initiatives are designed to motivate children to be active and #MakeMoves including encouraging them to invent unique skills and celebrations, which can be transformed into mascot animations using motion-capture technology.

Further extending his reach, Albärt has ventured into the virtual world with his own island in the popular Roblox game, Piñata Smashlings™. Here, he continues to engage young fans in their digital playground, inspiring them to carry their virtual activities into the real world to stay active and healthy.

Albärt has had a busy tournament, touring the host cities throughout Germany, meeting fans and supporting the teams. His mission is ambitious: to inspire ten million children across Europe to get active, as he follows in the iconic, oversized footsteps of previous mascots like Berni, Goaliath, Rabbit, and Kinas.

MOMENTS WORTH STOPPING FOR

INDONESIA

QATAR

BOOK YOUR QATAR STOPOVER NOW FROM 14$*

*Terms and conditions apply

visit QATAR

FUSSBALLLIEBE FINALE TAKES CENTRE STAGE

OFFICIAL MATCH BALL GIVEN FRESH NEW LOOK

A bespoke match ball has been produced by adidas for the UEFA EURO 2024 semi-finals and final: the FUSSBALLLIEBE FINALE.

The official match ball that the remaining teams going for glory will use sees a refresh of the iconic visual elements from the ball that kicked things off back on 14 June. The prominent black wing shapes have been accentuated with vibrant edges, curves and dots that take on the unmistakable black, red and gold of the host nation, Germany.

The white base is replaced with an eye-catching silver, representing the silverware that the teams will be competing for. The silver colour of the ball has been specially developed and tested with athletes to ensure that it stands out on the pitch without reflecting light back off the surface.

It will be the first ball used in a EURO final to feature Connected Ball technology – which delivers precise ball data to video match officials in real time. Combining player position data with AI, the innovation contributes to UEFA's semi-automated offside technology and has been key to supporting in-match decisions throughout the tournament.

The technology also enhances the overall fan viewing experience by offering accurate measurement of in-play data – including the ball speed, spin and distance the ball travelled before hitting the back of the net to watching fans.

The ball's CTR-CORE is designed for accuracy and consistency, promoting fast, precise play with maximum shape and air retention. The PRECISIONSHELL polyurethane (PU) skin features micro and macro textures and a 20-piece panel shape designed for enhanced aerodynamics.

As well as using recycled polyester and water-based ink, FUSSBALLLIEBE FINALE is made from more sustainable bio-based materials than any previous adidas official match ball. Every layer of the ball has been adjusted to include materials such as corn fibres, sugar cane, wood pulp and rubber.

FIRE IS SONG OF SUMMER

Italian electronic trio MEDUZA, GRAMMY® nominated OneRepublic, and German singer-songwriter Leony are the big names behind the official UEFA EURO 2024 song, called FIRE.

The song sits alongside the #LightYourFire campaign which invites fans globally to share their passion.

The three acts have brought their own touch to the track – and their own take on what it means to them: for MEDUZA, the song merges their love for football with their music, emphasising the unifying power of music amidst excitement for the tournament; OneRepublic's Ryan Tedder sees the song as an inspiration to unite fans worldwide; this echoes Leony's childhood love for football and her joy in contributing to the official tournament song.

'FIRE' embodies the spirit of football and music enthusiasts, blending MEDUZA's anthemic house production, OneRepublic's compelling soundscapes, and Leony's pop expertise into a celebration of unity and exhilaration. It serves as a timeless soundtrack for UEFA EURO 2024.

The artists perform the anthem live at the closing ceremony just before kick-off, adding to the event's finale. Additionally, MEDUZA have also created a full auditory experience, a series of compositions inspired by the anthem to enrich TV sequences, walk-on music for teams entering the pitch, and key moments like the trophy presentation, ensuring that the spirit of UEFA EURO 2024 resonates in every aspect of the event, uniting music and football.

An official playlist is available on streaming platforms, providing a backdrop to the tournament.

OLYMPIASTADION BERLIN

BERLIN BERLIN BERLIN BERLIN

HISTORIC VENUE GETS A BIG OCCASION TO ADD TO ITS LIST OF SHOWPIECE EVENTS

When the players who have earned the right to take part in the final of UEFA EURO 2024 walk onto the field, they will feel the weight of history on their shoulders.

As soon as they arrive at the stadium they will look around and know they have been transported to a venue of real significance.

Even players who have been to the Olympiastadion Berlin before, whether earlier in this tournament or further back in their careers, will recognise that this sporting cathedral is the right place for a match of such magnitude.

The site in Charlottenburg-Wilmersdorf had historically been used for sporting activities and so was a natural choice for the development of a national stadium.

The Olympiastadion was built by Werner March as part of a larger complex. The huge arena was part-buried in the ground and could hold around 100,000 people at the time of the 1936 Olympic Games.

One of the distinctive features of the stadium is the marathon gate, an opening at one of the ends which had a base for the Olympic flame built into it. Indeed, 1936 was the first year that the flame went on a journey to the venue before the start of the Games.

This Olympic Games was also the first to be broadcast on TV and radio so viewers and listeners would have been able to experience the incredible feats of Jesse Owens, who won gold medals in the 100m, 200m, 4x100m relay and the long jump.

An historical link with track and field had been established, which was strengthened when it hosted the the World Athletics Championship (2009) and the European Athletics Championship (2018).

At the former, Usain Bolt created a benchmark for sporting excellence, just as Owens had done 73 years earlier, as he set new world records in both the 100m and 200m, as well as winning a third gold as part of the Jamaica 4x100m relay team.

While the Olympiastadion Berlin has also played host to American football and baseball, it is football that it is best known for.

The German Cup final, known as the Tschammerpokal originally and now the DFB-Pokal, was first held there in January 1937 and made itself welcome at several stadiums before finding a permanent home at the Olympiastadion in 1985. The women's domestic cup final was also played there from 1985-2009.

In 1963, the stadium got its own regular residents when Hertha Berlin moved in, in time for the first Bundesliga season, and 11 years later it had the honour of hosting three matches at the 1974 FIFA World Cup.

By the turn of the century a facelift was required for the modern era, and the need was accentuated when Germany won the right to host the 2006 FIFA World Cup.

The lower ring was updated and boxes were added to the upper ring to improve the stadium's status as a multi-purpose arena, with a reopening ceremony held in the summer of 2004. There were concerts and football matches, and international contests returned that September with a friendly between Germany and Brazil.

The home World Cup two years later was a time of real pride for the whole country. Twelve venues were selected to host matches, with Olympiastadion Berlin staging six matches, including the final as Italy won the trophy.

And the showpiece football occasions didn't end there. In 2011 it was a fitting stage for Germany's opening match at the Women's World Cup and in 2015 the UEFA Champions League final between Barcelona and Juventus came to town.

The stunning backdrop and sporting heritage were put on display again in 2023 when the Special Olympics World Summer Games held a stunning opening ceremony there. Such is the setting and suitability for grand-scale events, some of the planet's biggest artists have held concerts there, including The Rolling Stones, Guns 'n' Roses, U2, Madonna and Bruce Springsteen.

Now the stadium has another huge occasion to add to its role of honour – and the players and fans should enjoy every minute.

OLYMPIASTADION BERLIN

OLYMPIASTADION BERLIN

CAPACITY:
71,000

HOME TO:
HERTHA BERLIN

UEFA EURO 2024 CITY AMBASSADOR:
KEVIN-PRINCE BOATENG

OLYMPIASTADION BERLIN

WHEN THE EYES OF THE FOOTBALL WORLD WERE ON OLYMPIASTADION BERLIN…

1974 FIFA WORLD CUP

Three matches were hosted at the World Cup in 1974, including all of Chile's appearances at the tournament.

While the games were hardly awash with goals, West Germany and East Germany were able to play a match each there. Paul Breitner got the only goal for West Germany against Chile, while the South Americans earned a 1-1 draw with East Germany.

WEST GERMANY 1 v 0 CHILE
(GROUP MATCH)

CHILE 1 v 1 EAST GERMANY
(GROUP MATCH)

AUSTRALIA 0 v 0 CHILE
(GROUP MATCH)

OLYMPIASTADION BERLIN

2006 FIFA WORLD CUP

The stadium saw its fair share of drama during six matches at the World Cup in 2006.

Brazil, Sweden, Germany and Ukraine won group matches there before the host nation won a quarter-final against Argentina by virtue of a penalty shoot-out.

Spot-kicks were needed to separate Italy and France in the final too, though the game is also remembered for Zinédine Zidane's red card in extra time before Fabio Cannavaro lifted the trophy.

◆

BRAZIL 1 v 0 CROATIA
(GROUP MATCH)

SWEDEN 1 v 0 PARAGUAY
(GROUP MATCH)

ECUADOR 0 v 3 GERMANY
(GROUP MATCH)

UKRAINE 1 v 0 TUNISIA
(GROUP MATCH)

GERMANY 1 v 1 ARGENTINA
(GERMANY WIN 4-2 ON PENS, QUARTER-FINAL)

ITALY 1 v 1 FRANCE
(ITALY WIN 5-3 ON PENS, FINAL)

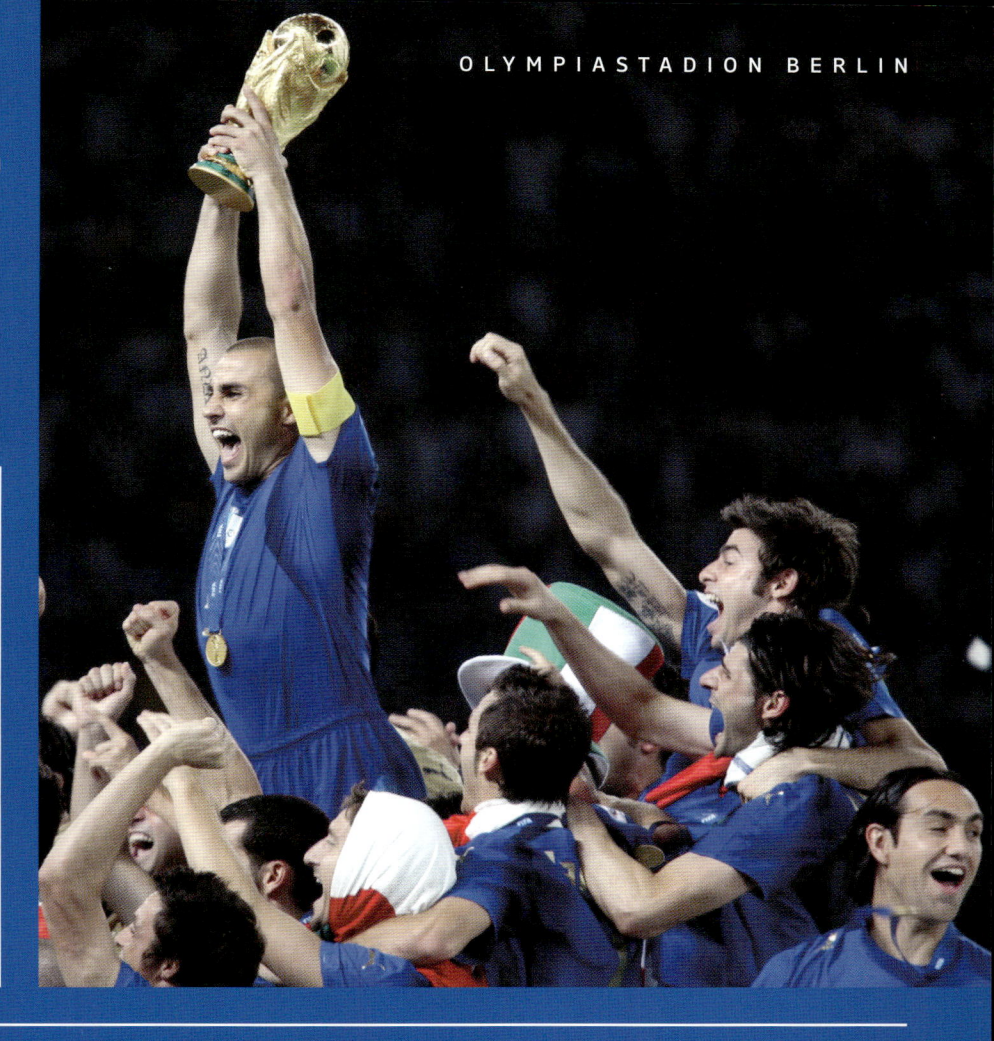

2011 FIFA WOMEN'S WORLD CUP

The largest of the venues at the Women's World Cup in 2011, the stadium was selected to host one of the tournament's biggest matches – the hosts' opener against one of the best sides of the era, Canada.

Two goals in the first half did the damage for Germany as Kerstin Garefrekes and Celia Okoyino da Mbabi found the net, but a Christine Sinclair free-kick made for an uncomfortable final 10 minutes for home fans.

◆

GERMANY 2 v 1 CANADA
(GROUP MATCH)

2015 UEFA CHAMPIONS LEAGUE FINAL

All roads led to Berlin for the 2015 UEFA Champions League final as Barcelona collected the trophy for the fifth time.

Ivan Rakitić finished off a fantastic team move to put the Catalans ahead, only for Álvaro Morata to equalise for Juventus.

Luis Suárez restored the lead before Neymar added a third in added time.

◆

JUVENTUS 1 v 3 BARCELONA

UEFA EURO 2024 OFFICIAL MATCHDAY PROGRAMME

MAKE A SAFETY STATEMENT

I DRIVE SLOW

OUSMANE DEMBELE
FOOTBALLER ICON

United Nations

Supported by **UEFA**

FINALS OF THE PAST

FINALS OF THE PAST

THE BEFORE, DURING AND AFTER OF THE MATCHES THAT HAVE DECIDED THE DESTINATION OF THE TROPHY

FINALS OF THE PAST

A GERMANY TREBLE

1972

PATH TO THE FINAL:
The final tournament was held in Belgium and consisted of two semi-finals before a third-place play-off and the final. A fierce strike by Anatoliy Konkov from the edge of the box settled the Soviet Union's semi-final with Hungary, while Gerd Müller enhanced his reputation further by scoring both of West Germany's goals in a 2-1 win over the host nation, who pulled one back through Odilon Polleunis.

FINAL RESULT:
WEST GERMANY 3 SOVIET UNION 0
Franz Beckenbauer was one of the biggest stars in world football in 1972 and it was he who took control of the final, striding out from the back to begin the move that ultimately led to Müller breaking the deadlock from close range in the first half. A fine move in the second period resulted in Herbert Wimmer advancing into the box and shooting across Yevhen Rudakov to double the lead before Müller completed the scoring with another predatory finish.

POST-MATCH:
It was Beckenbauer who stepped up to receive the trophy on behalf of his team at the Heysel Stadium. Müller, who finished top goalscorer with four, reflected: "The team was on a roll and we won. That final was the best of the lot."

WHAT HAPPENED NEXT...
It would be 1982 before the Soviet Union would qualify for their next major tournament, but West Germany, who had Beckenbauer, Müller and Günter Netzer making up the top three in the 1972 Ballon d'Or voting, were world champions two years later at a FIFA World Cup they hosted.

FINALS OF THE PAST

1980

PATH TO THE FINAL:
This was the first EURO that had eight teams in the finals as the winners of two four-team groups met each other in the final in Rome. West Germany beat holders Czechoslovakia and the Netherlands, and got a point against Greece to top Group 1, while Belgium finished on the same points and goal difference as Italy in Group 2 but progressed as they'd scored more goals.

FINAL RESULT:
WEST GERMANY 2 BELGIUM 1
Horst Hrubesch only managed six goals in his entire international career but two of them came in this year's final. His emphatic strike from the edge of the box gave West Germany the lead at the Stadio Olimpico and there were no further goals in an even contest until the final 15 minutes. René Vandereycken slammed in an equaliser from the spot before Hrubesch summoned up any remaining energy he had to power a header home from a corner with less than two minutes to go.

POST-MATCH:
"It was very hot that day and I recall being so tired after the game that it was hard to lift the trophy." That was the verdict from Hrubesch, recalling the sweltering June temperatures that day. His team-mate Klaus Allofs finished top of the goalscoring charts with three after his hat-trick against the Netherlands.

WHAT HAPPENED NEXT...
West Germany were among the favourites for the 1982 FIFA World Cup and made it to the final where a Paolo Rossi-inspired Italy took the title. Belgium made it as far as the second group stage.

1996

FINAL RESULT:
GERMANY 2 CZECH REPUBLIC 1
(after extra time)
Injuries and suspensions weakened the Germany side for the final but they could still call a match-winner from the bench to create history. Patrik Berger's penalty had given the Czech Republic the lead. With just over 20 minutes remaining Oliver Bierhoff was brought on and headed an equaliser a few minutes later. The game went to extra time and Bierhoff turned and shot to score the first golden-goal decider in a major tournament final.

POST-MATCH:
This was the first trophy Germany won following reunification and it was Jürgen Klinsmann who collected the silverware as captain. Matthias Sammer was named Player of the Tournament and team-mate Jürgen Kohler said they had prevailed because "mentally, we were beasts".

WHAT HAPPENED NEXT...
Germany qualified for the 1998 FIFA World Cup and made it as far as the quarter-finals before being knocked out by Croatia, while the Czech Republic next returned to major tournament action at EURO 2000, where they also lost to the eventual champions, France.

PATH TO THE FINAL:
Germany met the Czech Republic in their first group match at EURO '96 and their 2-0 win meant Berti Vogts' side topped Group C ahead of their Czech rivals. Germany overcame Croatia, then triumphed in a penalty shoot-out against England to reach the final, while the Czechs also needed penalties, against France, having overcome Portugal.

UEFA EURO 2024 OFFICIAL MATCHDAY PROGRAMME

FINALS OF THE PAST

GLORY FOR ITALY

1968

PATH TO THE FINAL:
Having made it to the finals in 1968 on home soil, Italy had a correct call of a toss of a coin to thank for making it through to the final, having drawn 0-0 in their semi-final with the Soviet Union. Goals were hard to come by in the other match too, but Yugoslavia dug deep to earn a 1-0 victory over England thanks to Dragan Džajić.

FINAL RESULT:
ITALY 2 YUGOSLAVIA 0
(Replay)
Fittingly, for such a tight tournament, it took a replay to separate the sides in the final. Džajić followed up his semi-final heroics by giving Yugoslavia the lead, only for Angelo Domenghini to fire a free-kick equaliser. Italy made a couple of changes for the replay, one of which was the return of Gigi Riva, who opened the scoring, before Pietro Anastasi volleyed a stunning second.

POST-MATCH:
Having won Italy's first EURO title, legendary goalkeeper Dino Zoff remembered how close his team came to losing the first final, saying: "To be honest, we didn't deserve to draw." Things were different in the second match and Giacinto Facchetti was the man who captained the side.

WHAT HAPPENED NEXT...
A fine Italy side went all the way to the FIFA World Cup final two years later but were beaten by one of the greatest ever Brazil sides. Yugoslavia failed to qualify for the finals.

FINALS OF THE PAST

2020

PATH TO THE FINAL:
A unique 60th anniversary tournament was spread across 11 different countries and Italy were able to get maximum points from three group matches in Rome before knocking out Austria, Belgium and Spain en route to the Wembley final. There they would meet England, who topped their own group before eliminating Germany, Ukraine and Denmark.

FINAL RESULT:
ITALY 1 ENGLAND 1
(Italy win 3-2 on penalties)
Having not won a major tournament since 1966, rising hopes of success went through the roof for England when Luke Shaw gave them the lead after only two minutes. Growing Italy pressure in the second half resulted in Leonardo Bonucci turning in an equaliser from close range and the game went to extra time, and then penalties. Although England goalkeeper Jordan Pickford made two saves in the shoot-out, it was Italy who prevailed 3-2.

POST-MATCH:
Giorgio Chiellini accepted the Henri Delaunay Cup on behalf of his victorious team and Italian newspaper Corriera dello Sport proclaimed: "The cup has returned home." Goalkeeper Gianluigi Donnarumma – who saved penalties in two shoot-outs – was named Player of the Tournament.

WHAT HAPPENED NEXT...
England picked themselves up to qualify for the next FIFA World Cup in 2022 where they reached the quarter-finals, while Italy's form tailed off and they lost in a play-off, therefore not making it to Qatar.

UEFA EURO 2024 OFFICIAL MATCHDAY PROGRAMME

From the everyday game to the beautiful game

Your offical partner for fresh fruit and vegetables

WE'RE ON YOUR TEAM

UEFA EURO 2024 GERMANY | Lidl — Official Partner

FINALS OF THE PAST

2016
PARTIES IN PORTUGAL

PATH TO THE FINAL:
Portugal didn't plot the most spectacular route to the final in France, drawing all three of their group games before an extra-time victory over Croatia, eliminating Poland on penalties and claiming their only win inside 90 minutes in the semi-final against Wales. In the final they would face the hosts, who had a more convincing journey, topping their group before beating the Republic of Ireland, Iceland and Germany.

FINAL RESULT:
PORTUGAL 1 FRANCE 0
(after extra time)
Portugal's hopes of a first major tournament win seemed to be in tatters when talisman Cristiano Ronaldo left the field injured in the first half. An entertaining match saw both teams strike the frame of the goal before the decisive moment arrived with just over 10 minutes of extra time remaining. Substitute Eder struck a low, hard shot past Hugo Lloris from the edge of the box and Portugal could celebrate their greatest moment in international football.

POST-MATCH:
Top-scorer Antoine Griezmann was named Player of the Tournament but it was Ronaldo who got his hands on the most important prize as he lifted the trophy on behalf of Fernando Santos' squad. France captain Lloris was magnanimous in defeat, saying: "We need to congratulate Portugal as they were very strong mentally throughout the tournament."

WHAT HAPPENED NEXT...
France used the disappointment as inspiration and Didier Deschamps led the side to FIFA World Cup glory in 2018 in Russia. Portugal made it to the knockout rounds before losing to Uruguay but went on to win the inaugural UEFA Nations League the following year.

1960
SOVIETS STRIKE FIRST

PATH TO THE FINAL:
France hosted the first EURO, known then as the European Nations' Cup, and the home side was involved in what remains the highest-scoring match in the competition's history, losing 5-4 to Yugoslavia in their semi-final. The Soviet Union had a much more comfortable route to the final, beating Czechoslovakia 3-0.

FINAL RESULT:
SOVIET UNION 2 YUGOSLAVIA 1
(after extra time)
With legendary goalkeeper Lev Yashin as the last line of defence and captain Igor Netto pulling the strings, the Soviet Union were in confident mood but found themselves behind at half-time following a goal credited to Milan Galić. The crowd at Parc des Princes saw Slava Metreveli equalise from close range and the decisive moment arrived in the second period of extra time as Viktor Ponedelnik headed in the winner.

POST-MATCH:
The delighted Soviet players enjoyed their celebrations in Paris after Netto had collected the trophy, though Yuriy Voynov admitted: "We didn't drink much. We were drunk on victory."

WHAT HAPPENED NEXT...
The success of the inaugural tournament put the European Championship on the path to continual growth and popularity. As for the first finalists, they were put in the same group at the 1962 FIFA World Cup. The Soviet Union topped the table but lost to Chile in their quarter-final while Yugoslavia finished second and reached the semi-finals.

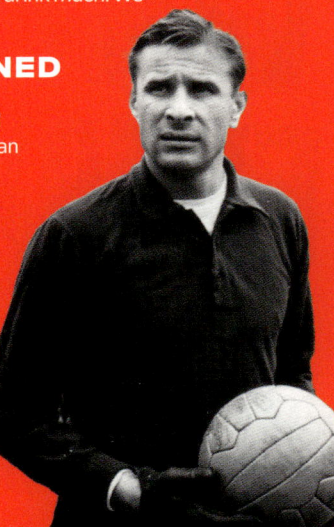

UEFA EURO 2024 OFFICIAL MATCHDAY PROGRAMME 53

THE TASTE YOU DESERVE
WHEN YOU CROSS EVERYTHING YOU CAN

Coca-Cola | UEFA EURO 2024 GERMANY

OFFICIAL PARTNER

©2024 The Coca-Cola Company. Coca-Cola, Coca-Cola Zero und die Konturflasche sind eingetragene Schutzmarken der The Coca-Cola Company.

FINALS OF THE PAST

DANISH SURPRISE

1992

PATH TO THE FINAL:
Denmark had failed to qualify for the final tournament, but were drafted in to replace the suspended Yugoslavia. Once there, victory in their final group game set up a semi-final which they won on penalties against the Netherlands. Germany finished second in Group 2, then beat Sweden 3-2 to reach the final in Gothenburg.

FINAL RESULT:
DENMARK 2 GERMANY 0
Denmark's emergence from the shadows to reach the final was already a fairytale, but in beating the mighty Germany to secure the trophy the achievement reached epic proportions. A goal in each half, the first a spectacular strike from the edge of the box by John Jensen, and the second an equally brilliant Kim Vilfort shot that went in off the post, did the damage.

POST-MATCH:
The result sent shockwaves throughout Europe and goalscorer Vilfort said: "We didn't have the best players, but we had the best team." Captain Lars Olsen collected the trophy and the celebrations continued back home. Goalkeeper Peter Schmeichel recalls: "It really sank in when we were in Copenhagen. That was unbelievable, truly unbelievable."

WHAT HAPPENED NEXT...
That day in 1992 remains the greatest in Danish football history. They failed to qualify for the FIFA World Cup two years later, while Germany reached the quarter-finals before losing out to Bulgaria.

What unites us matters.

That's why we're your partner.

Football unites us. This is where we share our passion, our values and a willingness to give it our all – no matter where we come from or whatever else we might believe in. That is why we are supporting the European Football Championship and its Volunteer Programme in our role as National Insurance Partner of UEFA EURO 2024™ and Partner of the German National Team. Together we want to turn this tournament in the heart of Europe into a football festival for everyone.

ERGO

Simple because it matters.

Official Partner of the German National Team & Official National Partner of UEFA EURO 2024™

FINALS OF THE PAST

CHEEK OF A CZECH

1976

PATH TO THE FINAL:
This was the last time a four-team finals took place and both semi-finals required extra time to produce a winner. Anton Ondruš scored at both ends for Czechoslovakia against the Netherlands before two goals in the added period sealed a 3-1 win. The following day West Germany recovered from 2-0 down before ultimately prevailing 4-2, thanks largely to a hat-trick from Dieter Müller.

FINAL RESULT:
CZECHOSLOVAKIA 2 WEST GERMANY 2
(Czechoslovakia win 5-3 on penalties)
Once again, West Germany gave themselves a mountain to climb by conceding the first two goals but Bernd Hölzenbein's late effort made it 2-2 and took the game to extra time, which didn't produce a winner. The crowd in Belgrade then witnessed something that has been replayed millions of times since. Knowing his spot-kick could decide the destiny of the trophy, Antonín Panenka had the courage and skill to chip the ball gently down the middle and settle the contest.

POST-MATCH:
"I am very proud of this penalty that is part of football history. It was definitely the highlight of my career." That's the verdict of Panenka when he looks back on the legacy of that penalty. The fact he scored allowed Ondruš to lift the trophy as the winning captain.

WHAT HAPPENED NEXT...
The 1976 UEFA European Championship is the only major tournament Czechoslovakia has won. They failed to qualify for the 1978 FIFA World Cup but came third in the next EURO. West Germany got to the second group stage at the World Cup before bowing out.

UEFA EURO 2024 OFFICIAL MATCHDAY PROGRAMME

FINALS OF THE PAST

FANTASTIC FRANCE

1984

PATH TO THE FINAL:
The common thread through France's entire route to the final was Michel Platini. The Juventus forward scored seven of France's nine goals in the group stage but took until the 119th minute of the semi-final to convert what proved to be the winner against Portugal. Spain's journey was less spectacular but a semi-final shoot-out victory over Denmark sent them to the Paris final.

FINAL RESULT:
FRANCE 2 SPAIN 0
France claimed their first international title and Platini ensured he had scored in all five of his team's games, though the opener against Spain wasn't one of his most aesthetically pleasing as his free-kick squirmed past Luis Arconada. A red card for Yvon Le Roux with five minutes to go increased French anxiety but Bruno Bellone settled the game in the closing moments.

POST-MATCH:
Platini's nine goals in five games remains the most a player has scored in a single finals. He triumphantly declared: "We were superior to everybody and expressed ourselves on the pitch." It was he who lifted the Henri Delaunay Cup, and he won the Ballon d'Or that year too.

WHAT HAPPENED NEXT...
Both France and Spain gave a good account of themselves at the 1986 FIFA World Cup, Spain reaching the quarter-finals while France finished third.

FINALS OF THE PAST

2000

FINAL RESULT:
FRANCE 2 ITALY 1
(after extra time)

The 2000 final is proof, if proof were needed, that you have to keep your concentration until the referee signals the game is over. Italy claimed the lead through Marco Delvecchio in Rotterdam and had the scent of victory in their nostrils before substitute Sylvain Wiltord grabbed an added-time leveller. That set the platform for David Trezeguet to become the hero, slamming in a fantastic goal for France's second golden goal of the tournament.

POST-MATCH:
Didier Deschamps became the second player – following Franz Beckenbauer – to captain a team to both World Cup and EURO glory, while the incomparable Zinédine Zidane was named Player of the Tournament. Noting his side's late goal that snatched victory away from Italy, France coach Roger Lemerre commented: "We said that if there is a second left we have to go all out for it. The miracle happened and we caused it."

WHAT HAPPENED NEXT…
From the high of being world and European champions, France came down to earth with a bump at the 2002 FIFA World Cup, finishing bottom of their group, while Italy lost out to hosts South Korea in the round of 16.

PATH TO THE FINAL:
France arrived at UEFA EURO 2000 as world champions and began confidently, though they lost their final group game to the Netherlands in Amsterdam. Spain were beaten in the quarter-finals before a golden goal was needed to dispatch Portugal. Italy topped their group before knocking out Romania and overcoming the Netherlands on penalties in their semi-final.

FINALS OF THE PAST

A SPAIN HAT-TRICK

1964

PATH TO THE FINAL:
The second European Nations' Cup was held in Spain and the hosts faced a tricky semi-final against Hungary which went to extra time following a 1-1 draw before Amancio settled the contest. The Soviet Union eased past Denmark in the other match 3-0.

FINAL RESULT:
SPAIN 2 SOVIET UNION 1
An early goal apiece suggested the final could be a classic at the Santiago Bernabéu as Spain opened the scoring only for the Soviet Union to equalise after eight minutes. The home side assumed control but it took until the 84th minute to find a winner through Marcelino's diving header.

POST-MATCH:
Ferran Olivella lifted the trophy in front of nearly 80,000 fans and goalkeeper José Ángel Iribar said: "When we won, we were full of joy, we were so into it."

WHAT HAPPENED NEXT...
Both teams made it to the 1966 FIFA World Cup, though the Soviet Union fared the better. They reached the semi-finals while Spain were eliminated at the group stage, resulting in the dismissal of coach José Villalonga.

2008

PATH TO THE FINAL:
The tournament was held in Austria and Switzerland, and Spain found the surroundings to their liking as they won all of their group games before knocking out Italy and Russia, though the quarter-final against the Azzurri went to a nail-biting shoot-out. Germany finished behind Croatia in their group, then had entertaining 3-2 wins against Portugal and Turkey to reach the final in Vienna.

FINAL RESULT:
SPAIN 1 GERMANY 0
For years Spain's fans thought a quarter-final curse prevented their team reaching the business end of major tournaments, so hopes were high when they made it to the final. As it was, it took just one moment to settle the match, which came in the first half when Fernando Torres latched on to a Xavi Hernández pass to clip the ball over Jens Lehmann and into the net. It was a goal that ended a 44-year wait for a major trophy.

POST-MATCH:
Iker Casillas became the first goalkeeper to captain a team to EURO success and the celebrations continued in Madrid. Luis Aragonés stepped down as coach following the win and reflected: "We have put together a group that plays well, that keeps the ball and mixes their passes very well and that is difficult to stop."

WHAT HAPPENED NEXT...
This success was the catalyst for further Spanish glory as Vicente del Bosque led them to wins at the 2010 FIFA World Cup and UEFA EURO 2012. Germany also performed consistently well in the years to come, reaching the semi-finals of the next two tournaments.

FINALS OF THE PAST

2012

FINAL RESULT:
SPAIN 4 ITALY 0

The group encounter between the two sides had finished 1-1 but any thoughts that this would be a similarly close game were soon eradicated. Spain were 2-0 up by half-time, thanks to goals from David Silva and Jordi Alba. Italy made changes to try and find a way back into the contest but late goals from Fernando Torres and Juan Mata added gloss to the scoreline, which was the biggest margin of victory in a EURO final.

POST-MATCH:
Fernando Torres had become the first player to score in two European Championship finals and he took the Top Scorer award, while Iker Casillas became the first captain to lift the trophy twice. Spain coach Vicente del Bosque described his country's continued success as "a great era for Spanish football".

WHAT HAPPENED NEXT...
Both teams qualified for the FIFA Confederations Cup with Spain coming runners-up and Italy finishing third, but the World Cup a year later was a disappointment as both countries exited at the group stage.

PATH TO THE FINAL:
Defending champions Spain kicked off the tournament with a target on their back but they dealt with the pressure superbly, topping a group that included the other eventual finalists, Italy. The closest Spain came to being ousted was at the semi-final stage where they beat Portugal on penalties, having already knocked out France. Italy also needed penalties in eliminating England before edging past Germany.

In diesem Sommer wird Hopfen und Malz gegrillt!

Mann, is' das 'ne Wurst!

Offizieller Nationaler Sponsor der UEFA EURO 2024™

FINALS OF THE PAST

GREECE'S GOLDEN MOMENT

2004

PATH TO THE FINAL:
It was considered a shock when Greece beat Portugal 2-1 in the opening match of UEFA EURO 2004. That result helped them to qualify from the group before sensationally toppling France and the Czech Republic to reach the final. Portugal recovered from that early loss to win the group, then beat England on penalties and the Netherlands in a semi-final.

FINAL RESULT:
GREECE 1 PORTUGAL 0
The stage was set. Playing in their home tournament with many of the continent's most successful teams eliminated, and with legend Luís Figo and budding star Cristiano Ronaldo in attack, all the ingredients were there for a Portuguese triumph. Greece didn't read the script. Their organisation and discipline laid the foundation while Angelos Charisteas headed in superbly for the only goal of the game.

POST-MATCH:
German coach Otto Rehhagel had become the first man to lead a side that didn't share his nationality to EURO glory. Theodoros Zagorakis lifted the trophy as captain and was named Player of the Tournament. He commented: "We proved once again that the Greek soul is, and always will be, our strength."

WHAT HAPPENED NEXT...
As glorious as this 2004 feat was, it didn't spark a period of sustained Greek success. They failed to qualify for the next FIFA World Cup and were knocked out at the group stage at the following EURO. Portugal reached the semi-finals and then the quarter-finals of the same tournaments.

UEFA EURO 2024 OFFICIAL MATCHDAY PROGRAMME

Betano
SPORTWETTEN

UEFA EURO 2024 GERMANY

OFFICIAL SPONSOR

OFFIZIELL LIZENZIERT (WHITELIST) | 18+ | SUCHTRISIKO | BUWEI.DE | AGB GELTEN

FINALS OF THE PAST

THE DAZZLING DUTCH

1988

PATH TO THE FINAL:
In some ways EURO '88 was a very simple tournament. There were no red cards, periods of extra time or penalty shoot-outs, and there were no goalless draws. There were two good teams in the final though and they met in the group stage. The Soviet Union's win over the Netherlands effectively sealed top spot in the group, but both safely qualified for the semi-finals where the Netherlands beat West Germany and the Soviet Union did likewise to Italy.

FINAL RESULT:
NETHERLANDS 2 SOVIET UNION 0
The second meeting of the two sides produced a very different result – and one of the reasons for that may have been the fact Marco van Basten had earned a place in the Dutch starting line-up by then. The tall striker would end the tournament as top scorer with five and his fifth strike was the best of the lot, volleying in spectacularly to seal a 2-0 win in Munich. Captain Ruud Gullit had put the Netherlands a goal up but the Soviet Union would rue hitting the post and having a penalty saved by Hans van Breukelen.

POST-MATCH:
After several near-misses, this was the first time the Netherlands had landed a major title – though attention on the overall achievement was somewhat overshadowed by the quality of Van Basten's famous goal. Coach Rinus Michels described it as "a goal more beautiful than the most ambitious script", while Van Basten himself said: "It was just a fantastic feeling."

WHAT HAPPENED NEXT...
Gullit remembers the journey back to the jubilant Netherlands. "We got on the plane and the captain had a nice idea to fly around over Eindhoven," he recalls. "Then we waved with the plane to everybody, like this [stretches arms out and dips one then the next]. I said, 'Just put us down, safe and sound, and then we can celebrate'." At the next major tournament, the 1990 FIFA World Cup, his side were beaten in the round of 16, while the Soviet Union failed to make it out of the group.

THE CITY OF BERLIN

THE BRILLIANCE OF BERLIN

'City of Freedom' it proudly says on the Berlin tourist board's website and there can be few cities in the world that embody the spirit of the global game as much as here.

The past century, in particular, has seen Berlin go through lots of changes, but the dividing of the city in the aftermath of World War II and the subsequent tearing down of the wall that had split the city in two has created a place that is a symbol of people coming together, just as football fosters unity.

What has emerged is a Berlin that embraces its past but looks to the future; a huge city that has multiple focal points and has lots to offer residents and tourists.

Germany's capital is welcoming and has a diverse population with creativity a major part of its identity, housing lots of varied museums to visit and an ever-evolving list of cultural events to attend.

It is also a very green city, symbolised by Tiergarten, an area of huge parks that encompass Berlin Zoo and have the Victory Column at its centre – a monument that was built around 150 years ago to commemorate the wars that united Germany and are now a symbol of peace.

Berlin is the most populous urban area in the country with around 4.5 million inhabitants. Its industry is largely based around the service sector, and the best way to get around is the S-Bahn, a train network that rides the rooftops of the city.

There are tourist attractions galore but the character of the place is found in its widespread neighbourhoods such as Kreuzberg, Prenzlauer Berg, Friedrichshain and Hackescher Markt with their cafés, bars, street acts and shops. There is no better place to experience Berlin's very own edible invention, currywurst.

It is all a far cry from Berlin's humble beginnings when the first settlements were created by German merchants towards the end of the 12th century on the banks of the River Spree, though 1237 is recorded as the city's date of foundation.

Berlin was made capital of the former empire of Prussia in 1701 and remained an important seat of power when the German Empire was established in 1871.

The World Wars of the 20th century took a huge toll but since the removal of the Berlin Wall, the city has regained its place at the heart of Germany and has rebuilt into the fascinating and wonderful place it is today.

FASCINATING FACT

◆

The Adlon Kempinski Hotel, near Brandenburg Gate, was the inspiration for the film Grand Hotel, which won the Best Picture Oscar in 1932 and is famed for Greta Garbo uttering the immortal line: "I want to be alone."

THE CITY OF BERLIN

FIVE THINGS TO EXPERIENCE IN BERLIN

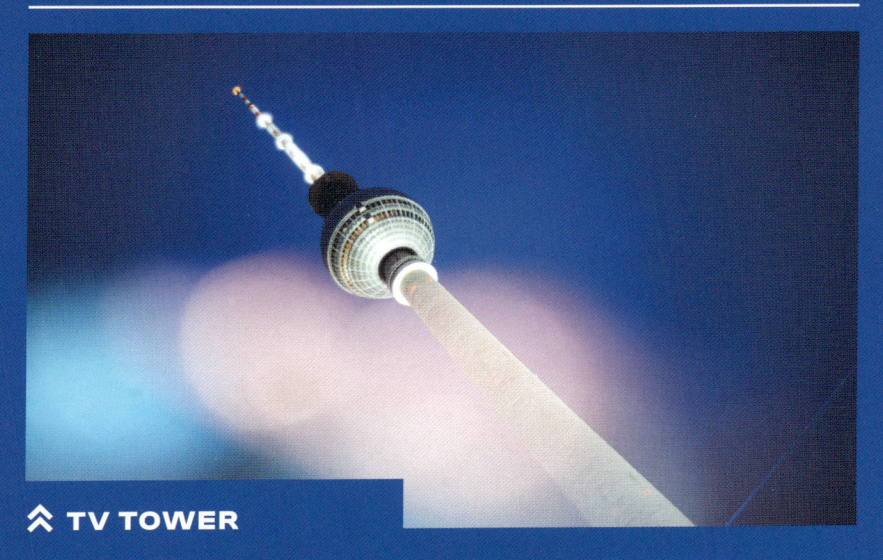

⌃ TV TOWER

Completed in 1969, the TV Tower, or Fernsehturm, stands at 368m and is Germany's tallest structure. Its primary function is as a television and radio transmitter but it has become a tourist attraction with a bar and observation deck that completes a full revolution once per hour. The express lifts take tourists to the top in under a minute.

⌃ MUSEUM ISLAND

Located on a small island on the River Spree, which was where the first Berlin settlements sprung up, Museum Island is a collection of five buildings housing five different collections. They are Altes Museum (Greek, Etruscan and Roman artefacts), Neues Museum (Egyptian collection), Alte Nationalgalerie (19th century European art), Pergamonmuseum (architecture from ancient worlds) and Bode-Museum (medieval sculptures).

⌄ REICHSTAG

The Reichstag is the centre of German politics, the place where the country's elected officials sit – and there is so much history attached to it. The building has seen some changes over the years, not least when a stunning glass dome was added to the top, allowing visitors great views over the city once they've ascended the spiralling ramp to the top.

⌃ CHARLOTTENBURG PALACE

A 10-minute drive from Olympiastadion Berlin is Schloss Charlottenburg, a grand palace that has expanded through the centuries since its original construction between 1695 and 1699. It was named after Sophia Charlotte of Hanover, the wife of King Frederick I, and has a distinctive dome, several extra buildings and an extensive garden. The place is dripping with history.

⌃ BRANDENBURG GATE

Built between 1788 and 1791, the Brandenburg Gate is a sandstone monument that came to mean much more than being a beautiful old building modelled on the Acropolis in Athens. It became associated with the East-West divide following World War II when the Berlin Wall was constructed around it. It then became the focus of joy and a symbol of unity when the wall was eventually removed in 1989.

UEFA EURO 2024 OFFICIAL MATCHDAY PROGRAMME

GERMANY'S PARTY

GERMANY'S PARTY

The party may be drawing to a close with only two teams left to compete for the trophy but every participating nation has brought its own colour and noise to UEFA EURO 2024.

A month-long celebration of the best that European football has to offer has been enjoyed, creating memories that will last forever.

However, the reality is that it is fans who turn a great event into a spectacular one, and supporters of each of the 24 countries involved should take a bow for creating such a fantastic atmosphere.

With their face paints, flags and unique costumes, here is a flavour of images that prove how crucial fans were to the party that Germany hosted…

GERMANY'S PARTY

GERMANY'S PARTY

70 UEFA EURO 2024 OFFICIAL MATCHDAY PROGRAMME

GERMANY'S PARTY

GERMANY'S PARTY

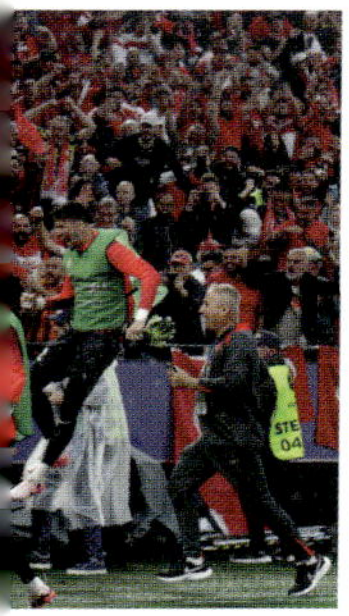

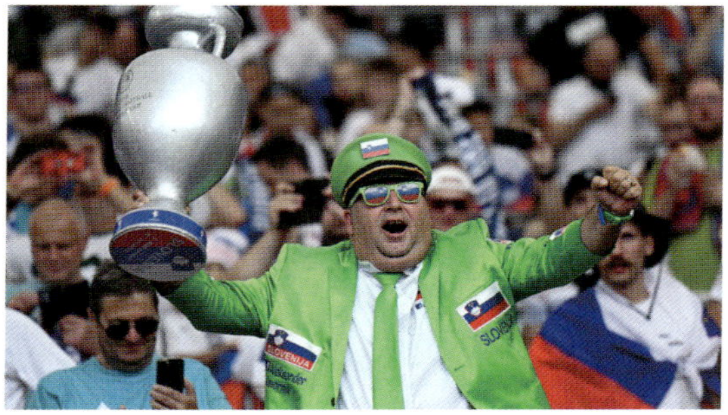

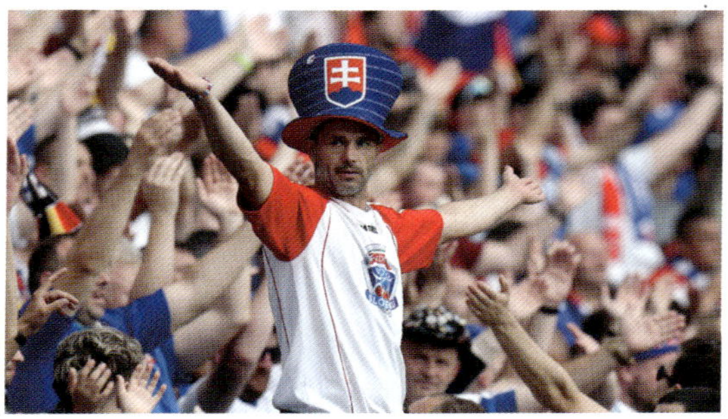

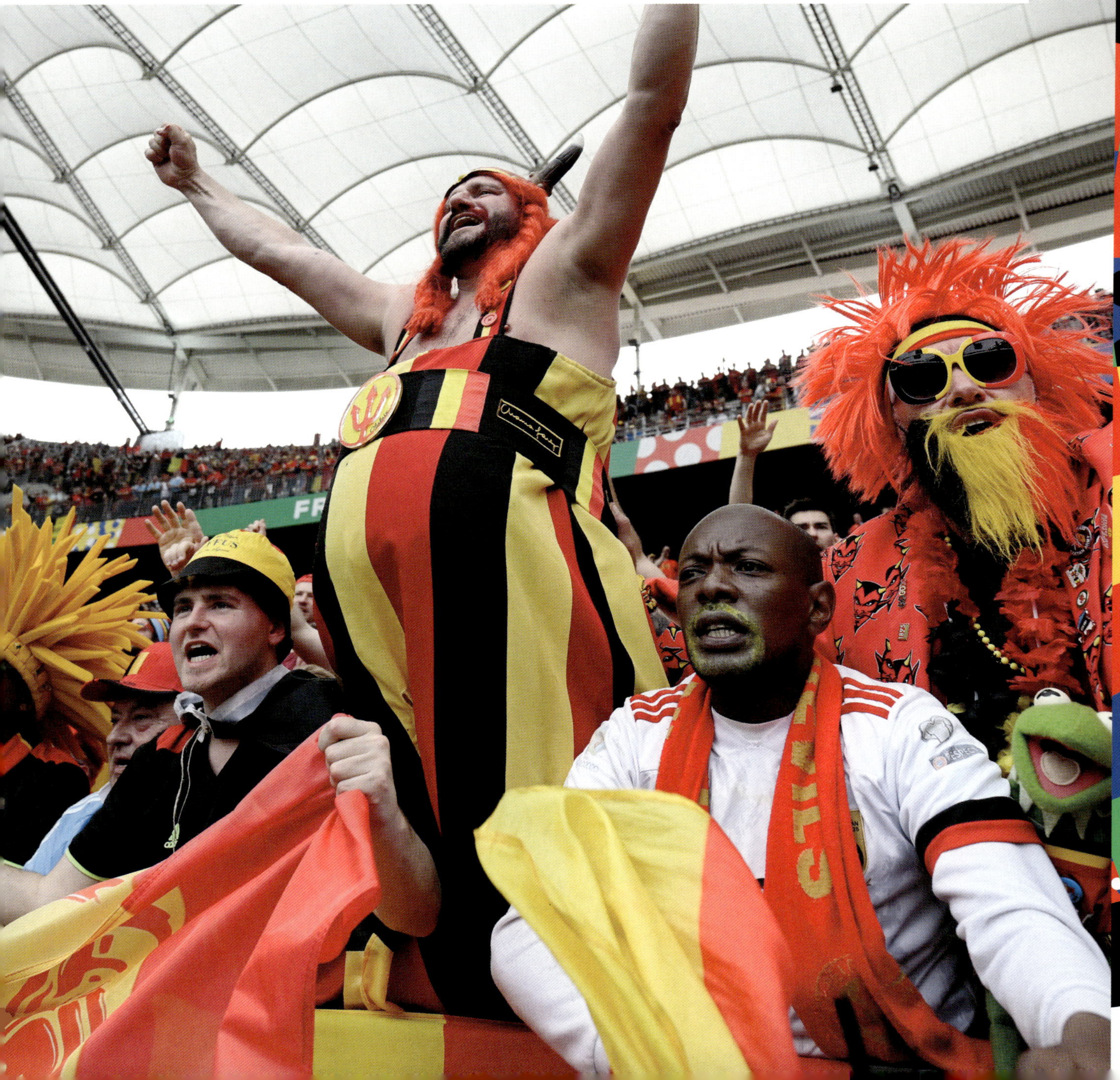

ENDLICH ANSTOSSEN

Bitte

Bitte ein Bit

UEFA EURO 2024 GERMANY | **Bitburger**

Offizielles Bier der UEFA EURO 2024™

WHAT'S IT LIKE TO REFEREE AT A EUROPEAN CHAMPIONSHIP?

WE SPEAK WITH BJÖRN KUIPERS, THE MAN IN THE MIDDLE FOR THE UEFA EURO 2020 FINAL, WHO HAS HELPED TO GUIDE THIS YEAR'S OFFICIALS THROUGH THE TOURNAMENT

There are few better ways to retire from the game than by being involved in a European Championship final.

That was the honour bestowed upon Björn Kuipers at EURO 2020, when the Dutchman was selected to referee the decider between England and eventual winners Italy at London's Wembley Stadium.

"It was a fantastic moment, one to never forget," Kuipers recalls. "I had refereed other finals but EURO was not on the list, so it was really something special and we got very positive feedback as a team of officials. I had already decided it would be my last game, I didn't want to be past my sell-by date, and it was the perfect moment to finish."

Kuipers is now a member of UEFA's referee committee, and is part of the support team that appointed officials for EURO 2024, helping to guide them through an intense period that began well before the tournament kicked off.

"If you are selected for the EURO, then you are one of the best referees in Europe, and therefore the world," Kuipers said pre-tournament. "It is a special honour, but it also means that you have to perform. When the referees come to Germany, the focus is completely on football and they will be prepared in the best possible way."

The matches come thick and fast, and just like players, referees eagerly awaited their match appointments. When selected, they have been officiating at the most technically advanced EURO yet, with connected ball technology added to VAR, semi-automated offside and goal-line technology for the first time.

VAR has been used carefully, with minimum interference to avoid only clear errors, while referees were instructed to be firm on dissent and unsporting behaviour.

"The most important thing is respect and fair play," said Kuipers. "The players and coaches are examples for young people, so they cannot react to decisions in an unacceptable way."

This message was communicated to coaches at a pre-tournament meeting, and Kuipers and his refereeing colleagues also visited squads ahead of the kick-off to discuss key issues.

UEFA's Be a Referee! campaign is inspiring young people across Europe to pick up the whistle and sample life as a match official.

We are looking to recruit 40,000 new referees each season to help support the running of the game at grassroots level. As well as a good understanding of the game, officials need a strong sense of fairness, impartiality and the ability to make quick decisions under pressure.

"To become a referee, you need to love football," says Björn Kuipers. "We want strong characters with good body language and a positive attitude."

Scan the QR code to find out more!

HOW UEFA REINVESTS EURO REVENUE INTO FOOTBALL DEVELOPMENT

This year marks the 20th anniversary of HatTrick, UEFA's flagship development programme.

Since its launch in 2004, UEFA HatTrick has evolved into one of global sport's largest solidarity schemes, channelling €2.6bn into football development programmes. By reinvesting men's EURO revenue back into the game through projects at national association level, it has become an important driver of UEFA's not-for-profit mission.

This year is a milestone one for HatTrick, not only because it marks its 20th anniversary, but also the start of a new cycle, its sixth. This one is set to redistribute more revenue than ever, with EURO 2024 projected to generate €935m – a 21% increase on the previous edition – for investment in football development projects across Europe over the next four years.

Before every HatTrick cycle is approved, UEFA engages in months of consultation with its 55 national associations to better understand the current footballing landscape and their changing needs. The last cycle is evaluated but also the previous cycles to spot longer term trends.

LEADING FACILITIES

One of the most significant ways in which HatTrick has transformed the European football landscape is through investment in infrastructure. By helping associations build new facilities and modernise existing ones, HatTrick has helped to level the playing field and strengthen the footballing pyramid across the continent.

At the very top level, HatTrick funding has contributed to

REINVESTING EURO FUNDS

the construction or development of 35 national stadiums, meaning more than 60% of national football grounds in Europe have been built or modernised thanks to the programme. This includes improvements in player and spectator safety, as well as improving accessibility for people with disabilities.

CASE STUDY: GEORGIA

To complement these stadiums, HatTrick investment has also helped construct 34 national training centres. The most recent of these can be found at first-time EURO final tournament qualifiers Georgia, where HatTrick funding contributed to the construction of five national training centres in the build-up to the European Under-21 Championship finals, co-hosted with Romania in the summer of 2023.

"The legacy of the tournament is invaluable for Georgian football," says Levan Kobiashvili, president of the Georgian Football Federation. "The newly built and renovated high-quality training and playing facilities are already serving

> "The legacy of the tournament is invaluable for Georgian football"

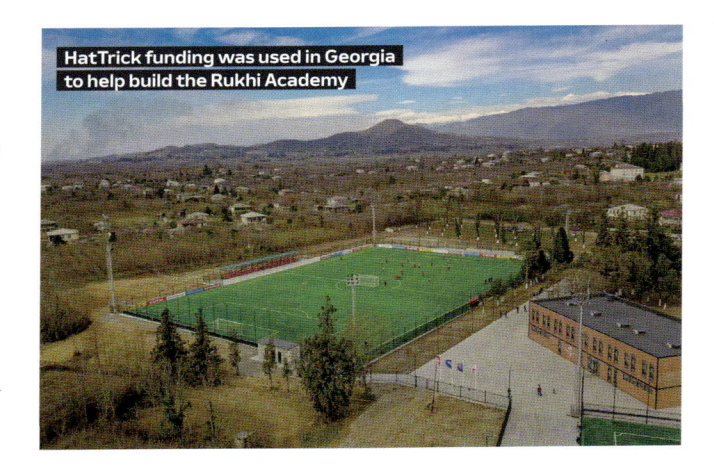

HatTrick funding was used in Georgia to help build the Rukhi Academy

to develop the domestic game." The results have already started to pay off as witnessed by the country's superb EURO finals debut this summer.

Looking further down the pyramid, HatTrick has funded thousands of playing pitches across the continent, ensuring everyone is given the chance to play football, regardless of where they live. More than 1,000 full-size and 3,000 mini pitches have been constructed with HatTrick funding since 2004, an average of more than 70 pitches per member association.

ACCELERATING DEVELOPMENT

Infrastructure is obviously an important aspect of HatTrick's impact, but the scheme also recognises the need to invest in the action on the pitch, not just the pitch itself. Over its 20 years of existence, HatTrick has funded more than 700 women's football development programmes, with nearly 60% of those projects creating new opportunities for women and girls to get into football. UEFA's investment in women's football has jumped by 50% since 2019, and HatTrick has played an important part in that increase.

More than 400 elite youth football projects have also been funded by HatTrick, helping associations develop talent pathways and raise the standards of youth coaching, while giving players the opportunity to compete at a higher level earlier in their careers. The Football in Schools programme, meanwhile, has reached 2.4 million children in more than 44,000 schools, with 100,000 teachers given training to deliver football sessions.

BROADER IMPACT

Away from the pitch, HatTrick has funded more than 500 social and environmental projects, helping to leverage football's influence as a wider force for good. As part of these efforts to tackle football's climate impact, recent HatTrick-funded schemes have addressed waste reduction, renewable energy transition, sustainable construction, and public transport uptake, among many others. Socially, HatTrick has funded projects aimed at eliminating discrimination, improving mental health, supporting refugees, safeguarding children, and many more.

When HatTrick was launched in 2004, few would have foreseen the depth and breadth of its impact on the European football landscape over the next 20 years. The sixth cycle of HatTrick will undoubtedly be bigger and better than ever, and with it, so will football.

1988 REWIND

A SUMMER OF FOOTBALL NOBODY COULD FORGET HAD WEST GERMANY AS THE PERFECT HOSTS – BUT A SPECIAL TEAM CARRIED OFF THE TROPHY

Think of the 1988 UEFA European Championship and images of Marco van Basten will immediately come to mind against an orange backdrop of excited Dutch fans – but there was much more to the tournament than that.

Apart from several matches as part of the pan-European UEFA EURO 2020, the eight-team tournament in 1988 was the last time a EURO was held on German soil.

Nearly 900,000 fans attended the matches as the public in West Germany enthusiastically supported the competition that was held across eight different cities – Cologne, Düsseldorf, Frankfurt, Gelsenkirchen, Hamburg, Hanover, Munich and Stuttgart.

One team they didn't get to see in action were the reigning champions, France, who were eliminated in the qualification stage, finishing behind the Soviet Union and East Germany in their group.

The eight teams that did make it to the finals were packed with quality as hosts West Germany prepared to share the stage with seven group winners – Denmark, England, Italy, Netherlands, Soviet Union, Spain and EURO debutants Republic of Ireland.

It was West Germany's neighbours and rivals, the Netherlands, who would ultimately carry home the trophy, though the tournament didn't begin quite as they would have liked.

Here's how EURO '88 unfolded…

1988 REWIND

MAGICAL MATCHES GROUP 1

Roberto Mancini was the first goalscorer in the first match of the tournament for a youthful Italy side as they took on West Germany in Düsseldorf.

Closing down doggedly in their opponents' half, Italy won the ball back and when the chance fell to Mancini inside the box, he drilled a low shot home.

The hosts didn't wait long to reply as an indirect free-kick was awarded near the edge of the box and Andreas Brehme struck the ball through the wall. In the days of two points for a win, both sides had to settle for one each.

The following day an action-packed game saw Spain defeat Denmark 3-2.

Michel proved too hot for the Danes to handle as he opened the scoring but Michael Laudrup equalised with a superb goal.

Troels Rasmussen saved a Michel penalty but he was powerless to prevent Emilio Butragreño and a Rafael Gordillo free-kick opening up a two-goal advantage before Flemming Povlsen struck late with a superb header.

That victory was as good as it got for Spain. They had high hopes coming into the tournament but Gianluca Vialli's excellently-worked goal decided the encounter with Italy and two goals from Rudi Völler ensured a 2-0 victory for West Germany in Munich.

Top spot in the group was cemented by that win for Franz Beckenbauer's side, who had beaten Denmark 2-0 in their second game thanks to goals from Jürgen Klinsmann and Olaf Thon.

Italy also progressed from the group, beating Denmark 2-0 in their third match, second-half goals from substitutes Alessandro Altobelli and Luigi De Agostini doing the damage.

GROUP 1 RESULTS

West Germany 1-1 Italy
Denmark 2-3 Spain
West Germany 2-0 Denmark
Italy 1-0 Spain
West Germany 2-0 Spain
Italy 2-0 Denmark

GROUP 1 TABLE

	P	W	D	L	GD	Pts
West Germany	3	2	1	0	+4	5
Italy	3	2	1	0	+3	5
Spain	3	1	0	2	-2	2
Denmark	3	0	0	3	-5	0

STRAUSS.COM
NOW SHIPPING GLOBALLY

UEFA EURO 2024 GERMANY

STRAUSS

OFFICIAL UEFA EURO 2024™ WORKWEAR PARTNER

HIGH-VIS – TEAMWEAR
AMBITION

STRAUSS WORKS WORLDWIDE

1988 REWIND

MAGICAL MATCHES GROUP 2

The Netherlands' first match didn't go to plan, but may just have been the wake-up call they needed.

A stubborn Soviet Union side limited opportunities for Rinus Michels' men while at the other end a superb strike from Vasiliy Rats settled the contest.

That goal did prompt the introduction of 23-year-old Marco van Basten from the bench and the striker would go on to have a telling contribution for the rest of the tournament.

In the other opening match in the group, the Republic of Ireland enjoyed a memorable first match at a EURO as Ray Houghton's early header settled the contest against England.

That result meant England's next match against the Netherlands would be a must-win for both teams, and it was that man Van Basten who stole the show.

England hit the post twice before a lovely turn and finish by Van Basten opened his account. Bryan Robson scored a delightful equaliser but the Netherlands' new hero struck twice more to claim a hat-trick in a 3-1 win and put his team back in the mix for qualification – which they sealed when Wim Kieft's strike was enough to beat the Republic of Ireland 1-0 in their last group game.

The Dutch had to settle for second place in the group though as the Soviet Union went unbeaten. After their opening win against the Netherlands, Oleh Protasov earned a point against the Irish after Ronnie Whelan's volley had put Jack Charlton's men ahead.

The USSR sealed top spot with a 3-1 win against England. Sergei Aleinikov, Oleksiy Mykhaylychenko and Viktor Pasulko scored the goals in Frankfurt, with Tony Adams replying.

GROUP 2 RESULTS

England 0-1 Republic of Ireland
Netherlands 0-1 Soviet Union
England 1-3 Netherlands
Republic of Ireland 1-1 Soviet Union
England 1-3 Soviet Union
Republic of Ireland 0-1 Netherlands

GROUP 2 TABLE

	P	W	D	L	GD	Pts
Soviet Union	3	2	1	0	+3	5
Netherlands	3	2	0	1	+2	4
Rep of Ireland	3	1	1	1	0	3
England	3	0	0	3	-5	0

1988 REWIND

CRUNCH TIME – THE KNOCKOUT ROUNDS

Four of Europe's big-hitters met in the semi-finals and the heavyweight clash between West Germany and the Netherlands was the main event for home fans.

The Dutch camp were motivated by thoughts of what had happened between the two countries 14 years earlier at the 1974 FIFA World Cup when West Germany won the final and the hosts would have hoped for a similar result when Lothar Matthäus squeezed in a second-half penalty.

The Netherlands were given a chance to level from the spot and Ronald Koeman made no mistake, leaving the stage set for Van Basten to write another chapter in his 1988 fairy tale by sliding and guiding a winner into the net with only two minutes remaining.

The match-winner said: "The game in Hamburg was a very special match for us because winning against Germany, especially in Germany, is not a thing that happens often."

The following day the Netherlands discovered that it would be the Soviet Union that they would face in the final.

Valeriy Lobanovskyi's men had struck a nice balance between defensive solidity and attacking threat and carried that into their last-four encounter with Italy.

A tight match in a rain-sodden Stuttgart burst into life in the second period as Gennadiy Lytovchenko showed great footwork to weave his way through the penalty area before slotting home, and four minutes later Protasov swept in following a swift counter-attack to set up a re-match with the Netherlands.

Nearly 63,000 spectators in Munich saw history made on 25 June as the Netherlands

1988 REWIND

finally stepped out of the shadows to claim a major trophy for the first time.

The Soviet Union had enjoyed a fabulous tournament but were undone in the final by one great goal, and one spectacular goal.

Van Basten ensured that 1988 would be remembered as his EURO by, first of all, leaping to nod the ball in Ruud Gullit's direction, the skipper doing the rest with a powerful header.

Then, when Arnold Mühren looped a cross towards the right-hand byline, Van Basten watched it all the way, then unleashed a volley from the tightest of angles over Rinat Dasaev.

There was still time for a scare for the Dutch when the Soviet Union were awarded a penalty but Hans van Breukelen made a brilliant save from Igor Belanov.

Gullit got to lift the Henri Delaunay Cup and later explained: "[The USSR] were in good shape too so it was a tough game. But then we scored through Van Basten – if he hit it a million times, he would never ever score that goal again."

Marco van Basten holds aloft the Henri Delaunay Cup that his five goals had helped to win for the Netherlands

> "If he [Van Basten] hit it a million times he would never score that goal again"
>
> — Ruud Gullit

SEMI-FINALS
Soviet Union 2-0 Italy
West Germany 1-2 Netherlands

FINAL
Soviet Union 0-2 Netherlands

TOP SCORERS
5 Marco van Basten
2 Oleh Protasov, Rudi Völler

UEFA EURO '88 FACT
The Netherlands' Hans van Breukelen, Ronald Koeman, Berry van Aerle and Gerald Vanenburg all won the EURO within weeks of lifting the European Cup with PSV.

TEAM OF THE TOURNAMENT

Hans van Breukelen (NED)

Giuseppe Bergomi (ITA)　Frank Rijkaard (NED)　Ronaldo Koeman (NED)　Paolo Maldini (ITA)

Giuseppe Giannini (ITA)　Jan Wouters (NED)　Lothar Matthäus (GER)

Gianluca Vialli (ITA)　Marco van Basten (NED)　Ruud Gullit (NED)

Günstig reisen mit den Sparpreisen.

bahn.de/sparpreise

Ab 12,99 €*

*Solange der Vorrat reicht. Im DB Fernverkehr (ICE, IC/EC). Buchbar bis 30.09.

UEFA's environmental, social and governance strategy covers various sustainable development goals

CLIMATE FUND LEAVES A EURO 2024 LEGACY

In the lead-up to this summer's tournament, UEFA launched a climate fund which gave German amateur football clubs and regional associations the opportunity to apply for environmental projects support.

The fund, which was announced under the slogan 'United by Football – Together for Nature', had a total of €7m earmarked for distribution. Clubs were able to suggest projects relating to one or more of the following four categories: energy, water, waste management and mobility.

As Michele Uva, UEFA social & environmental sustainability director, explains: "UEFA's climate fund offer has inspired thousands of grassroots clubs all over Germany, confirming the appeal of the programme and showing the acceleration potential of this initiative. The investment of €7m will contribute to a sustainable legacy for the EURO 2024 tournament, making a significant impact on reducing CO_2 emissions and supporting climate protection. It's great to see our environmental, social and governance strategy further coming to life, catalysing actions in support of the environment."

The fund was an instant hit following its launch on 8 January with thousands of clubs in Germany submitting applications. Popular projects included the installation of LED floodlights, photovoltaic solar panels, smart irrigation system, sharing stations for e-cars and heat pumps.

Major efforts have been made to reduce the environmental impact of the tournament through the targeted measures and investments laid out in the UEFA EURO 2024 ESG strategy.

€7M IS HELPING GERMAN AMATEUR FOOTBALL CLUBS TO DEVELOP ACTION PROJECTS

The €7m total is based on €25 being donated for each tonne of CO_2 emissions predicted to be produced in connection with UEFA EURO 2024. This significant investment in projects that will mitigate CO_2 emissions over the long term will strengthen UEFA EURO 2024's legacy both within the German football community and for the environment.

Funding applications were able to be requested for any sum up to a maximum of €250,000 with clubs only having to finance a maximum of €5,000 or 10% of the total project costs themselves. A simplified application procedure applied to requests for less than €25,000, and applicants were allowed to combine various smaller projects in a single application.

More information: www.uefa.com/sustainability/euro2024climatefund

"It's the first time that a climate fund has been set up for a EURO tournament. It's a great investment for the sake of our climate and in our football infrastructure in Germany. On behalf of the entire German football family, we would like to thank UEFA for the initiative and its implementation"

Heike Ullrich, German Football Association (DFB) general secretary

UEFA EURO 2024 GERMANY

BEHIND THE SCENES AT THE FINAL

UEFA EURO 2024 is the result of years of detailed preparation. Discover some key activities that go into organising the biggest football match of the tournament – the final at Berlin's Olympiastadion.

Venue operations

25 operational areas with over **90** staff involved in delivering the match

Media operations

1,000 TV/radio commentators and reporters in the media tribune

160 photographers pitchside

Volunteers

1,600 volunteers support stadium and host city operations, including ticketing, spectator services and fan zones

Pitch management

Grass cut to a standard height of **22mm** on matchday to guarantee best playing conditions

Accessibility

Special seats reserved for disabled supporters

Multilingual audio-descriptive commentary for blind and partially-sighted fans

Host broadcasting

46
TV cameras provide live coverage to over **200** territories worldwide

Recycling

Stadium dressing and signage items will be converted into new products after the EURO

Hisense | UEFA EURO 2024 GERMANY

OFFICIAL PARTNER

Beyond Glory

HOW TO WIN A EURO

HOW TO WIN A EURO

THE LAST COACH TO LEAD A TEAM TO THE TITLE OF EUROPEAN CHAMPIONS, ROBERTO MANCINI, EXPLAINS HOW ITALY FORGED A PATH TO GLORY

Everybody sets out to win, but at what point did you think you could go all the way at UEFA EURO 2020?
"I always believed it was possible to win – I believed it from day one. But there are lots of other factors as well. We knew what we were doing, even during the qualification phase, and we believed it was possible to do something special. The teams who played in the EURO were all very strong and they all wanted to win, so there was a good balance. There are many strong teams in Europe. Winning wasn't a simple task."

What were the key moments?
"We really believed in what we had done in the lead-up to the EURO but, of course, the important – crucial – match was the first.

UEFA EURO 2024 OFFICIAL MATCHDAY PROGRAMME   89

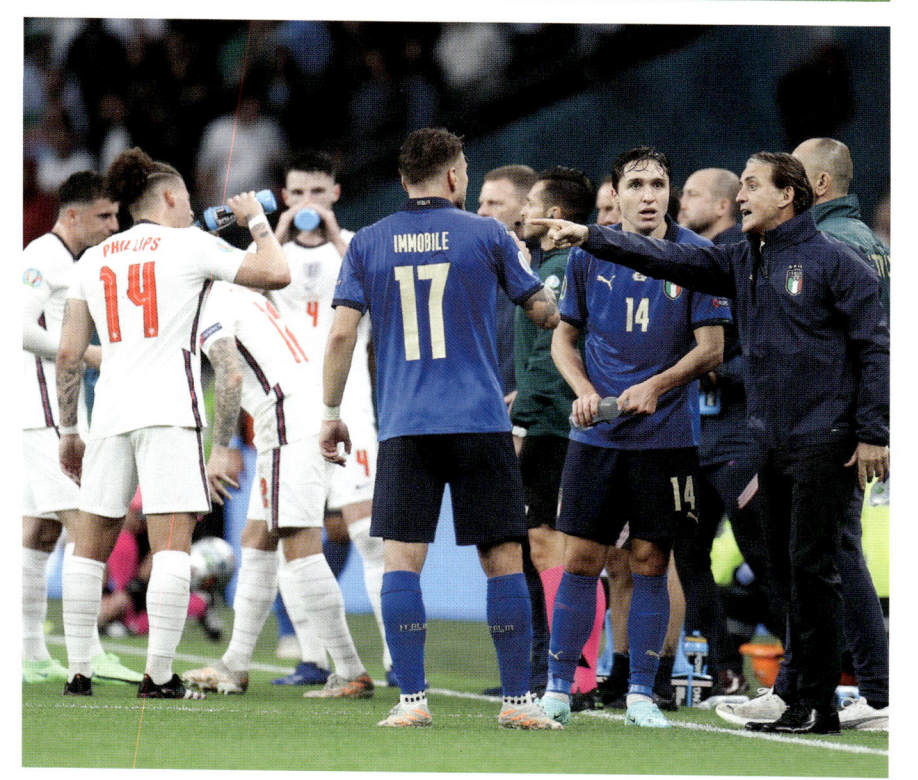

In a knockout competition, the first is always the most difficult. But then when you settle into it, it becomes different."

Maybe the performance against Belgium [in the quarter-finals] showed your confidence and physical condition?
"That was a very important match. The final against England was a great match, too. We suffered a bit more against Spain, because they played probably their best match of the whole tournament and they are a very strong team. I think that, from the round of 16 onwards, they were all great matches. There are some games when you have to suffer. Spain surprised us at the start by deciding to play without a striker. They caused us a lot of trouble and we had a hard time because we didn't have much of the ball."

How important was team spirit? And what did you do to create it?
"They did well because they formed a good group of guys – great guys first and foremost, which was essential. Plus, the more experienced players helped the younger players to integrate. That was also quite simple, and they deserve a lot of credit for creating a group that really wanted to play good football. It's not that I felt everything would be easy because there are always difficulties, but we made it. We were together for 50 days, which was tough, but I have to say that it all went fast. That's a sign that the guys got on well with each other."

You also implemented a more positive style, focused on attacking. Was that difficult to do?

HOW TO WIN A EURO

"It was actually quite simple, because I found players who wanted to do something special. They were enthusiastic about the project because it was something different for them. They were curious to see what we Italians could do. Obviously it took some time, but not that much. Whenever we got to see each other, it went well because they got something special out of it."

Italy were able to adapt to different opponents. How did you manage to prepare different tactical systems?
"It was a group effort. We tried to work on different ways of playing as well as the physical fitness side. We tried to improve our qualities as individuals and as a team. We succeeded, all together – us, the staff and the players, because they showed a lot of desire."

How important was it that you could make five or six substitutions [for the first time at a EURO]?
"I think it was important for everyone because the players had all just come off the end of an exhausting season, so I think it was a very good thing. We'd been working as a group for a long time and the guys who came off the bench knew what to do. Indeed, I have to say that whenever they came on, they gave something more, because when a tired player came off, a fresh player came on with a desire to improve the team – and that's not always the case. I have to say they were excellent, everyone, every time – in each game, those who came on did something special. It's important that the identity of the team remains the same even when we change three or four players. They all know what to do and the end product does not change."

Is there a lesson that EURO 2020 taught you?
"That you never give up until the end. It's not something we learned at EURO 2020, but it's something that was confirmed there. When you play, you should always believe in your abilities and your qualities because every match starts 0-0, and then you never give up for any reason because, in today's football, you can always make a comeback."

> **"You should always believe in your abilities because every match starts 0-0, and then you never give up for any reason"**

BYD | EURO 2024 GERMANY

UEFA EURO 2024™ Official Partner

BYD SEAL U DM-i
Super DM Technology

| **Up to 1080 km** | **18.3 kwh** | **5.9 s** |
| Combined range | Battery capacity | AWD 0–100 km/h |

byd.com

BUILD YOUR DREAMS

GET TRAINED SAVE LIVES

Just like Albärt, you can learn how to save a life. Scan the QR code and join a fun online course now!

UEFA

EUROPEAN RESUSCITATION COUNCIL

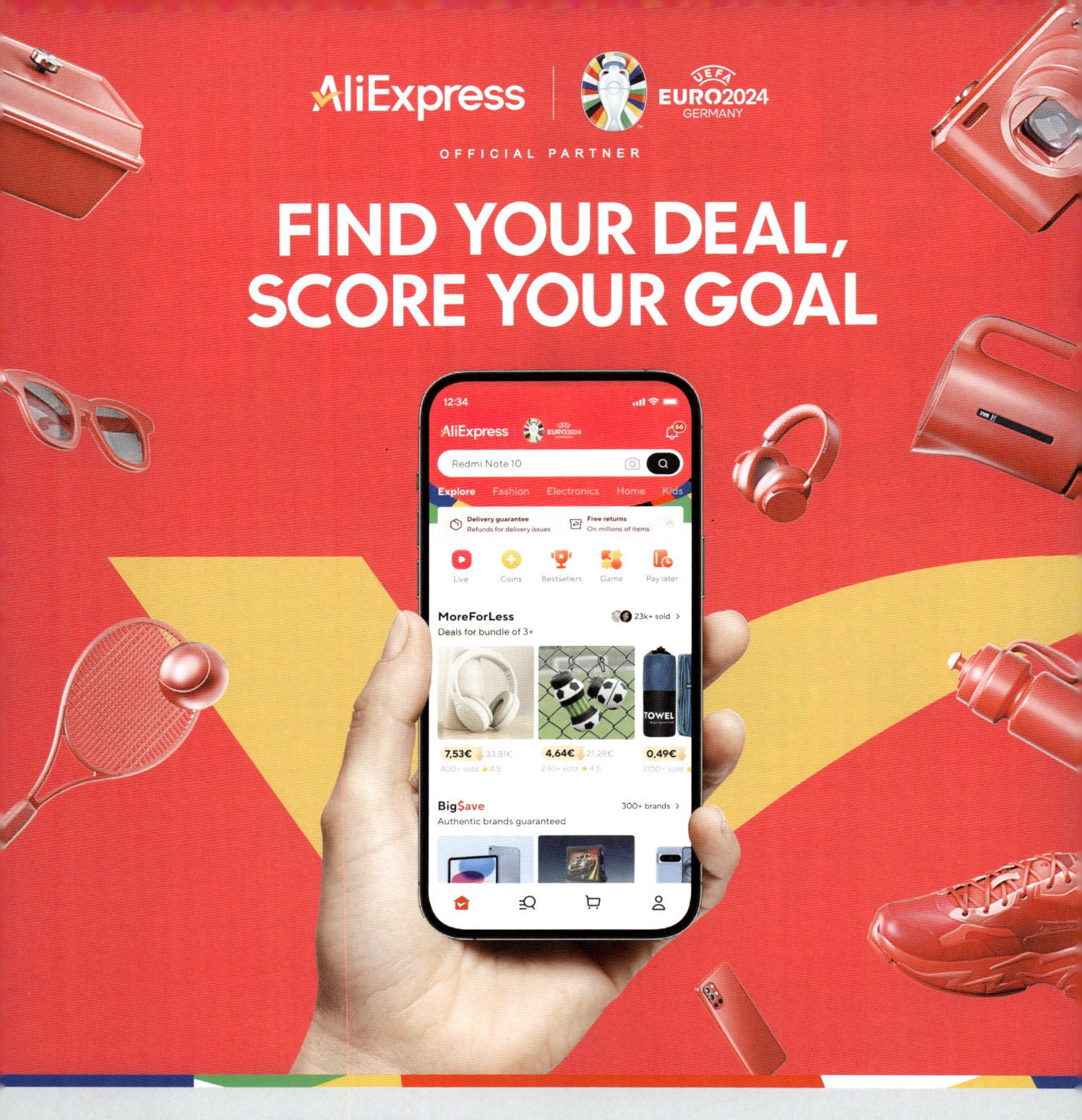

AliExpress | UEFA EURO 2024 GERMANY
OFFICIAL PARTNER

FIND YOUR DEAL, SCORE YOUR GOAL

What is AliExpress?

As the first exclusive e-commerce platform partner for a UEFA Men's European Football Championship, AliExpress will connect online consumers with this summer's festival of football offering amazing deals and interactive game prizes.

Download the App

'GET TRAINED, SAVE LIVES': GIVING FOOTBALL FANS CPR SKILLS

UEFA and the European Resuscitation Council (ERC) have teamed up to educate more than 100,000 fans in basic CPR skills and provide in-person training to teams, officials, volunteers and staff at UEFA EURO 2024.

The campaign, 'Get trained, save lives', is being backed by Erling Haaland, Lautaro Martínez, Ana Marković, Ruud Gullit, Gareth Bale, Thierry Henry, Didier Deschamps, Manuel Neuer and Rio Ferdinand. A dedicated platform teaching football fans the basic skills of cardio-pulmonary resuscitation (CPR) in under four minutes has been set up at get-trained.com.

The CPR training on this interactive training module is set in a virtual dressing room and sees Gullit invite football fans to join Haaland, Martínez, Bale, Henry, Ferdinand and Marković on the course. As it commences, interactive questions guide users through the teaching material, with players reacting to and commenting on their answers.

'Get trained, save lives' is part of UEFA's commitment to ensuring the highest standards of medical care and preparedness within football. Since last year, UEFA's minimum medical requirements stipulate that no UEFA match can start without an advanced life support ambulance and three automated external defibrillators (AED) on-site.

Sudden cardiac arrest is the third leading cause of death in Europe, happening to one in 1,000 people every year. In this situation, every minute that passes decreases the chances of survival by 10%. That is why CPR training is so important. Someone nearby when a person suffers a sudden cardiac arrest needs to be able to act quickly to save a life. Getting medical assistance and CPR immediately is crucial because every second counts.

UEFA and the ERC have so far provided hands-on training to 3,000 players, coaches, referees, officials and staff at finals and tournaments. In the build-up to EURO 2024, all participating teams learned how to provide first aid in case of a sudden cardiac arrest.

The campaign has received extra attention during EURO 2024, with a TV commercial and activities in all fan zones across the ten host cities.

"The focus of our campaign launched jointly by UEFA and the ERC is on the power of bystanders – everyday heroes who can turn critical moments into stories of hope and survival. Even a simple chest compression within the first few minutes following a cardiac arrest can significantly increase survival chances and reduce the risk of long-term damage. So, get trained and save lives. These words are the essence of our shared mission and our hope for a healthier, safer, and more compassionate society"

— UEFA President Aleksander Čeferin

QUIZ

TEST YOUR EURO KNOWLEDGE

1. Two UEFA European Championship finals have been decided by penalty shoot-outs. Which ones?

2. Which coach led West Germany to victory at EURO 1972 and the 1974 FIFA World Cup?

3. In which French stadium was the inaugural final held in 1960?

4. When Jürgen Klinsmann captained Germany to victory in the 1996 final, which club was he representing at the time?

5. Who was in goal for Italy when they became European champions in 1968?

6. Which Brazilian was Portugal coach when they reached the final in 2004?

7. The referees for both the 1960 and 1964 finals were from the same country, but which one?

8. Which midfielder was named man of the match when Spain beat Italy in the 2012 final?

9. Which West German made his 100th international appearance in the 1976 final?

10. Which midfielder struck his first international goal when he opened the scoring in the 1992 final?

11. Which West German winner of the 1980 EURO won the Ballon d'Or that year too?

QUIZ

MISSING TEAM-MATES
Can you guess which three names are missing from Germany's starting line-up from the final of EURO '96?

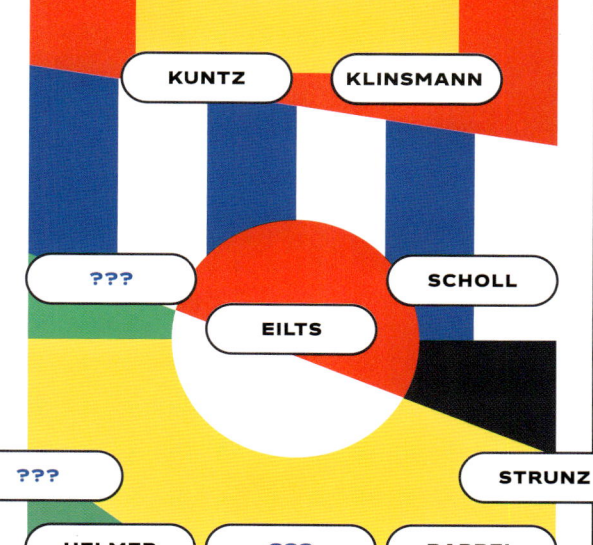

[Formation diagram with: KUNTZ, KLINSMANN, ???, SCHOLL, EILTS, ???, STRUNZ, HELMER, ???, BABBEL, KÖPKE]

12. Who stepped down as Spain coach after his team's success in the 2008 final?

13. Michel Platini's goal in the 1984 final took his tally to a record-breaking nine for the tournament, but who was the only other French player to register more than one goal?

14. Which defender was named man of the match when Portugal claimed victory in the 2016 final?

15. The Netherlands had a set of brothers in the line-up that won the 1988 final. Who were they?

YOUNGEST TO OLDEST
Can you put these EURO final goalkeepers in order of age – youngest to oldest?

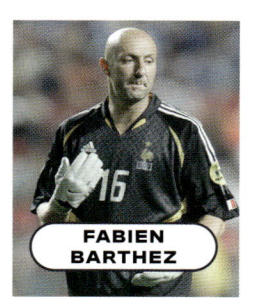

JENS LEHMANN | IKER CASILLAS | RICARDO | FABIEN BARTHEZ | GIANLUIGI BUFFON

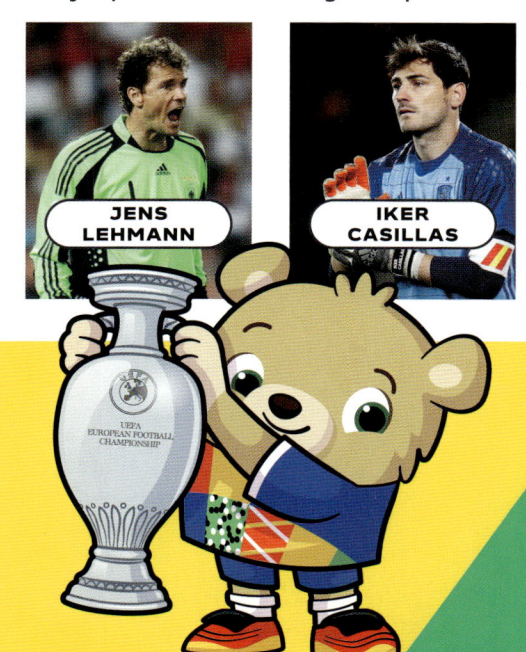

ANSWERS:
QUIZ: 1. 1976 & 2020, 2. Helmut Schön, 3. Parc des Princes, 4. Bayern München, 5. Dino Zoff, 6. Luiz Felipe Scolari, 7. England (Arthur Ellis and Arthur Holland), 8. Andrés Iniesta, 9. Franz Beckenbauer, 10. John Jensen, 11. Karl-Heinz Rummenigge, 12. Luis Aragonés, 13. Jean-François Domergue, 14. Pepe, 15. Erwin and Ronald Koeman.
MISSING TEAM-MATES: Sammer, Ziege, Häßler
YOUNGEST TO OLDEST: Casillas (born in 1981), Buffon (1978), Ricardo (1976), Barthez (1971), Lehmann (1969)

UEFA EURO 2024 OFFICIAL MATCHDAY PROGRAMME

UEFA EURO 2024 MATCH SCHEDULE

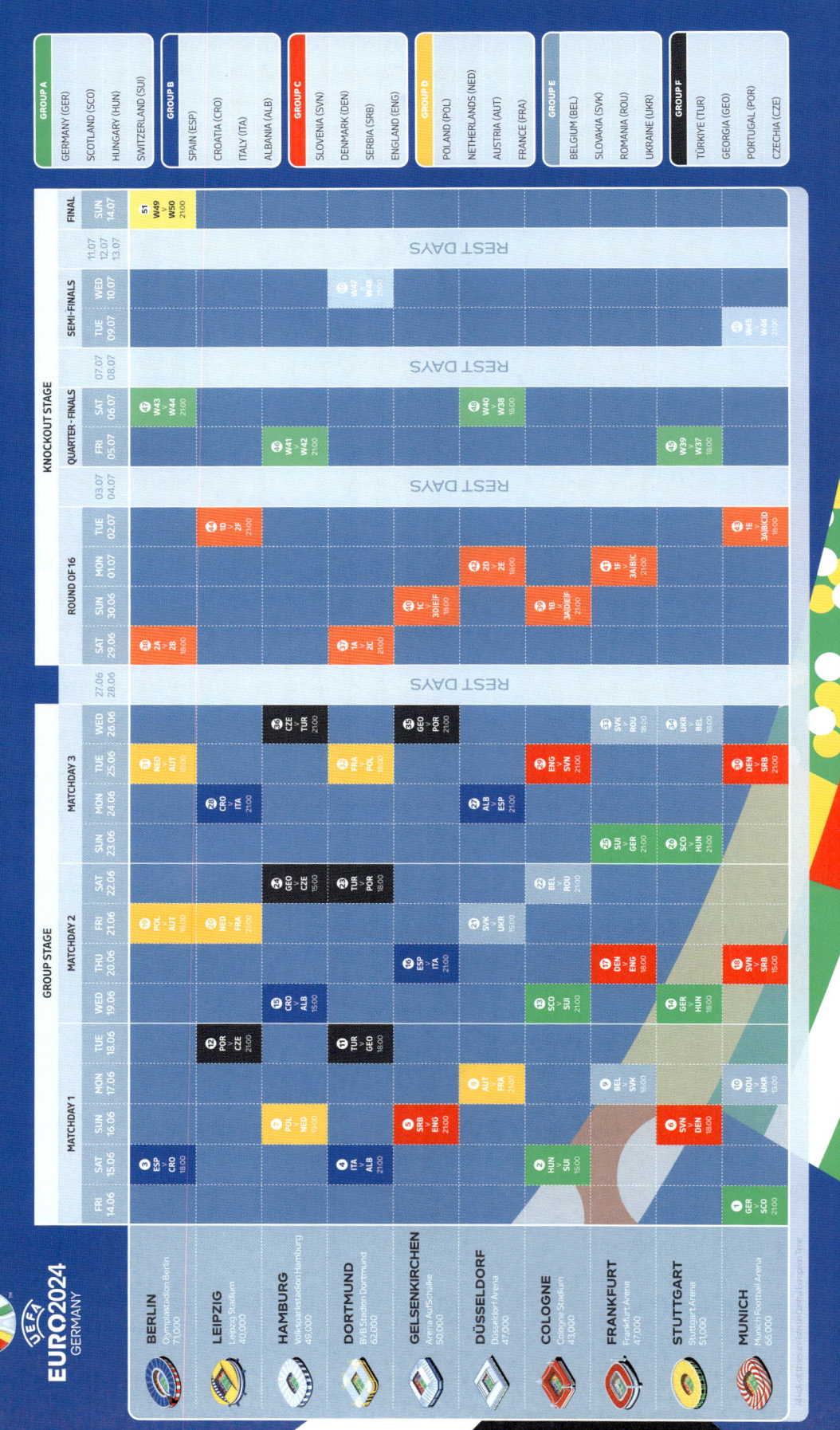

Groups

GROUP A
- GERMANY (GER)
- SCOTLAND (SCO)
- HUNGARY (HUN)
- SWITZERLAND (SUI)

GROUP B
- SPAIN (ESP)
- CROATIA (CRO)
- ITALY (ITA)
- ALBANIA (ALB)

GROUP C
- SLOVENIA (SVN)
- DENMARK (DEN)
- SERBIA (SRB)
- ENGLAND (ENG)

GROUP D
- POLAND (POL)
- NETHERLANDS (NED)
- AUSTRIA (AUT)
- FRANCE (FRA)

GROUP E
- BELGIUM (BEL)
- SLOVAKIA (SVK)
- ROMANIA (ROU)
- UKRAINE (UKR)

GROUP F
- TÜRKIYE (TUR)
- GEORGIA (GEO)
- PORTUGAL (POR)
- CZECHIA (CZE)

Venues

- **BERLIN** — Olympiastadion Berlin, 71,000
- **LEIPZIG** — Leipzig Stadium, 40,000
- **HAMBURG** — Volksparkstadion Hamburg, 49,000
- **DORTMUND** — BVB Stadion Dortmund, 62,000
- **GELSENKIRCHEN** — Arena AufSchalke, 50,000
- **DÜSSELDORF** — Düsseldorf Arena, 47,000
- **COLOGNE** — Cologne Stadium, 43,000
- **FRANKFURT** — Frankfurt Arena, 47,000
- **STUTTGART** — Stuttgart Arena, 51,000
- **MUNICH** — Munich Football Arena, 66,000

Group Stage

Matchday 1

Venue	FRI 14.06	SAT 15.06	SUN 16.06	MON 17.06	TUE 18.06
Berlin					
Leipzig		ESP v CRO 18:00			POR v CZE 21:00
Hamburg					
Dortmund		ITA v ALB 21:00			
Gelsenkirchen			POL v NED 15:00		
Düsseldorf				AUT v FRA 21:00	
Cologne					TUR v GEO 18:00
Frankfurt				BEL v SVK 18:00	
Stuttgart			SRB v ENG 21:00		
Munich	GER v SCO 21:00				

Also: HUN v SUI 15:00 (Cologne, 15.06); SVN v DEN 18:00 (Stuttgart, 16.06); ROU v UKR 15:00 (Munich, 17.06)

Matchday 2

Venue	WED 19.06	THU 20.06	FRI 21.06	SAT 22.06
Berlin		ESP v ITA 21:00		
Leipzig				
Hamburg			POL v AUT 15:00	
Dortmund				TUR v POR 18:00
Gelsenkirchen				GEO v CZE 15:00
Düsseldorf				
Cologne	SCO v SUI 21:00			BEL v ROU 21:00
Frankfurt		DEN v ENG 18:00		
Stuttgart				
Munich				

Also: CRO v ALB 15:00 (Hamburg, 19.06); SVK v UKR 15:00 (Düsseldorf, 21.06); NED v FRA 21:00 (Leipzig, 21.06); GER v HUN 18:00 (Stuttgart, 19.06); SVN v SRB 15:00 (Munich, 20.06)

Matchday 3

Venue	SUN 23.06	MON 24.06	TUE 25.06	WED 26.06
Berlin			NED v AUT 18:00	
Leipzig		CRO v ITA 21:00		
Hamburg				CZE v TUR 21:00
Dortmund			FRA v POL 18:00	
Gelsenkirchen		ALB v ESP 21:00		GEO v POR 21:00
Düsseldorf				
Cologne	SUI v GER 21:00		ENG v SVN 21:00	
Frankfurt				SVK v ROU 18:00
Stuttgart	SCO v HUN 21:00			UKR v BEL 18:00
Munich			DEN v SRB 21:00	

Rest Days: 27.06 – 28.06

Round of 16

SAT 29.06	SUN 30.06	MON 01.07	TUE 02.07
㊵ 2A v 2B 18:00	㊶ 1C v 3D/E/F 18:00	㊸ 2D v 2E 18:00	㊺ 1D v 2F 21:00
㊷ 1A v 2C 21:00	㊵ 1B v 3A/D/E/F 21:00	㊹ 1F v 3A/B/C 21:00	㊻ 1E v 3A/B/C/D 18:00

Rest Days: 03.07 – 04.07

Quarter-Finals

FRI 05.07	SAT 06.07
㊼ W39 v W37 18:00	㊾ W43 v W44 21:00
㊽ W41 v W42 21:00	㊿ W40 v W38 18:00

Rest Days: 07.07 – 08.07

Semi-Finals

TUE 09.07	WED 10.07
㊿ W45 v W46 21:00	㊿ W47 v W48 21:00

Rest Days: 11.07 – 12.07 – 13.07

Final

SUN 14.07 — 51 W49 v W50 21:00